SIMPLY REAL EATING

SIMPLY REAL EATING

Everyday Recipes and Rituals
for a Healthy Life Made Simple

SARAH ADLER

Photographs by Carina Skrobecki

THE COUNTRYMAN PRESS
A division of W. W. Norton & Company
Independent Publishers Since 1923

To my sweet family, dear friends, and the entire Simply Real Health community: this book is for you. Thank you for your endless love, encouragement, and support, and for allowing me into your kitchens and daily lives, in ways big and small. I hope this book brings you years of vibrant health, happiness, and the best memories around your table with the people you love the most.

And to Kyle, my forever and once-in-a-lifetime love and the best recipe tester around. And to my sweet Noah James: this book will always be the one that we made together.

For information about permission to reproduce selections from this book, write to Permissions, The Countryman Press, 500 Fifth Avenue, New York, NY 10110

For information about special discounts for bulk purchases, please contact W. W. Norton Special Sales at specialsales@wwnorton.com or 800-233-4830

Manufacturing by ToppanLeefung
Book design by Anna Reich
Production manager: Devon Zahn

The Countryman Press
www.countrymanpress.com

A division of W. W. Norton & Company, Inc.
500 Fifth Avenue, New York, NY 10110
www.wwnorton.com

978-1-68268-411-5

10 9 8 7 6 5 4 3 2 1

Right: Gluten-free Blackberry Scones, page 86

CONTENTS

Introduction   7

Getting Started   13

7 Steps to Creating a Healthy Lifestyle That Lasts   13
About This Book   18
Setting Up, Pantry Meals, and Meal Planning   20

MORNING MAGIC   27

NOURISHING NOONS   97

EFFORTLESS EVENINGS   147

SWEETS AND SIPS   221

Conversions   266
Index   268

INTRODUCTION

Truth: Food has always been *a thing* in my life.

At times, it's been one of my big loves; and at others, it's been an uphill battle: one filled with frustration, confusion, and information overload. But one thing is for sure: from as early as I can remember, I have always been completely obsessed and fascinated with the idea of living a healthy life.

At the age of seven, there was almost nothing I loved more than going to the natural food store to pick out my healthy cereal and snacks for the week.

By middle school, as other kids were collecting two-dollar bills, and makeup, I began to collect all the books and information about healthy eating that I could find: old college nutrition textbooks, diet books, fitness and health magazines, you name it. I consumed them the way other girls read teen magazines: with fervor, cuddled up, and secretly so no one would tease me.

By 15, I had read almost every book on nutrition out there, and had started using my body as a test case to try out all the different food theories. It was always just for fun back then, and because I truly loved it. But my innocent love of health started to become more of an unhealthy obsession. I became fixated with strictly following all the diet rules, eating perfectly, and never missing a workout.

My perfectionist tendencies started taking over the rest of my life. I dreaded Friday night sleepovers full of pizza and candy, going out to eat with people who happily devoured their burgers and fries while making fun of my plain salad, or traveling, because it messed up my perfect and healthy routine.

In college, things only got worse as I had less and less control over my food and daily schedule. I'd try to work out more ("calories in, calories out!" echoing in the back of my mind as I bounced on the treadmill) and became fixated on each new trend or diet. For four years straight, I'm pretty sure I survived on cereal with soy milk, nonfat yogurt, oatmeal, protein bars, popcorn, and frozen low-cal burritos.

Back then, food always lurked in the back of my mind: something to be battled against, controlled, and always aware of. It always felt like a lot of work—so much time and energy and planning—just to be healthy.

But, truthfully, I didn't have much to show for all that effort. No matter what I tried or did, my body never changed that much. I always had those "last five" I was determined to lose. My skin still had breakouts. I craved sugar after meals. Mentally, I was always looking for and fixated on shortcuts and work-arounds: how could I fool my sweet tooth or trick my body into never being hungry or magically burning more fat?

All of that changed my junior year, when the universe lovingly intervened: I got news that I had been accepted into a study-abroad program to Italy. And instead of feeling pure joy and excitement, all I could do was panic.

Italy. The land of pizza and pasta. Where gelato and wine were daily occurrences. And where there were exactly zero gyms, workout classes, or running shoes allowed. To everyone else, this was all part of the magic—but to me, all it did was give me anxiety. What would I do? What would I eat? And most important, and what I wouldn't say out loud:

how much weight would I gain? I almost didn't go on the trip.

By some act of grace, I ended up boarding the plane. I had a suitcase packed full with as many of my high-fiber protein bars as possible, my Nikes, and all my willpower and determination to beat the Italians and their pizza game. And it was a good thing I prepared, I remember thinking. Because Italy was exactly like I thought it would be. The rumors were true: they really did eat pizza and pasta every day, walked instead of worked out, and had wine and gelato the way we guzzled coffee in Seattle: at or in between every meal, and without a second thought.

I remember sitting in a piazza one afternoon, across from two beautiful Italian women catching up for lunch. They were sitting with their faces tilted to the sun, chatting with each other, as their plates of pasta and salad sat piled high in front of them. They slowly swirled their glasses of wine and laughed.

I sat, fascinated, and watched. They would slowly take bites of their pasta, twirling and talking, sipping and pausing. Calmly. Serenely. And so extremely present with each other, and in the moment. There was zero frantic energy, no pushing food around with their forks, no asking the waiter to please box up half of their food to go, and no talk of the carbs on their plates or the sugar in their wine, or being "bad" that afternoon.

Suddenly, it hit me so hard. I realized that I had never had a meal like that in my life: so peaceful, joyful, and in tune with who I was with, instead of consumed by the thoughts in my head. I could never just *be* or *just enjoy* a meal. My brain always felt full and occupied: always thinking about food. I was always calculating, making deals with myself about what to eat or not eat, how "good" or "bad" I was being, or what I would have to adjust to balance things out later. Of course, there was no room

for the joy I was witnessing—that delight, that pleasure, that pure enjoyment of food. My head-space was already too crowded.

I sat there, with my half of pizza pushed to the side of my plate and my plain water beside it.

I want what they're having.

It was the first moment I realized that having more joy with food didn't have to mean gluttony. It didn't mean you had to not care about your body and how you felt. But it did mean there was a lot more to the picture than I had thought. There was something else involved, a secret that these women were in on. Thoughts filled my head, as I sat there. *But, wait, how?! Like, seriously, how were they doing that? How did they look so good while eating all the foods I had been taught were the worst you could eat?*

I spent the rest of my trip determined to find out. The more I observed, the more I noticed that it wasn't just those two women—it was everyone in Italy. *It must just be the food*, I thought. *It's different here. More magical.* And, yes, that was true.

The food was simple. It was all fresh and pure. It was all homemade and homegrown. It was all real food, made from scratch.

But that wasn't all. It was the *way* they were about their food, too. And the role it played in their daily lives: it was a celebrated, sacred, and treasured part of life, meant to be enjoyed. Food was something to be restored and revived by. It was a pause in the day, to just be. To connect. To love and to share with others. It was something they happily made the space for in their days, not something they were inconvenienced by or rushed through. Food was a pillar in their life—a value, instead of an afterthought. They treated it, and their time spent with it and those they loved, with so much more beauty and respect than I had ever seen.

When I arrived back home, I decided to give it a try. To be like an Italian. To ignore all the noise, all the numbers and counting and measuring and obsessiveness, and just do as they did: eat simple, real food when they were hungry. I made it my goal to eat food that my body could more easily process, no matter the category or kind it was. And to try my hardest to just keep it as simple as that.

And so, it began. I swapped out my nonfat milk for a splash of real cream in my morning coffee and traded in my so-called healthy cereals for nutrient-dense vegetable-powered smoothies. I tossed out the packaged bars, and let myself eat a whole avocado with sea salt and pepper or an apple and peanut butter if I needed a midday snack.

I realized things like wine, coffee, chocolate, potatoes, and butter were actually real foods that had long traditions of artisan crafting, and that when they were made well, they were made with just a few pure ingredients. They were things not to feel guilty about, but to curate well and savor more intentionally in life.

Truthfully, it was hard—all my old programming and all the outdated diet rules kept popping into my head, trying to convince me that being this simple and relaxed about food would make me gain weight.

But after a few weeks, I started to notice something else entirely: I felt completely different. My energy level and appetite felt more stable and day by day, my cravings started to disappear. So many of the things I had considered "normal"—needing coffee to feel awake in the morning, needing wine to wind down at night, my slow digestion, craving sweets after lunch, skin breakouts—were fading quickly, if not already gone.

A whole new world of food options was suddenly fair game on the table, and it was actually starting to be fun to explore and try new things. But the best part of all? Without the restrictive and calculated diet rules, mentally, I also felt more free. I felt lighter, and clearer than I had in years. I felt energized, but also calmer and more grounded. I felt more balanced and steadier, instead of up and down and all over the place throughout the day. Those tiny annoying voices telling me what I should and shouldn't be eating slowly quieted down. Week by week, it felt as though my headspace had started to detox itself. As if there was more room and space and light in there, and that I had more capacity to focus on other things in life and be more present.

From that day in Italy forward, my life was changed. Instead of wasting any more energy or time on what the latest trends and fads were, I committed to eating real food, or as close as I could possibly get, as my new normal. And in place of the silly rules and quick-fix strategies, there was just one now: as long as I could recognize the ingredients, it was good to go.

It felt like I had found a special and secret power source to get more done in the day, be happier, and be able to handle so much more in life—whatever came my way. A new woman was born.

HOW I STARTED COOKING

It was only after the realization that what I ate directly affected how I showed up in my life, that I started to be interested in cooking at all. At first, it was out of necessity. Because let's be real: once I shifted to eating all real food, my "healthy" frozen meals and bars just weren't going to cut it any more.

How hard could it be? I just needed fresh food,

a little olive oil, sea salt and pepper, and to do as the Italians do. Before then, learning to cook, and trying to do it consistently, had felt very intimidating to me. Every time I had tried in the past, there were so many intricate rules. It was like a secret insider language to decode.

Motivated by how different my body felt when I ate real food, I started anyway, slowly and unsure of myself at first. But, started, nonetheless.

I looked at my shelf of healthy cookbooks for inspiration. But quickly, I became impatient at the long list of ingredients, exotic spices, buying bunches of herbs and using just a tiny snip, and the hour-long commitments for just one dish.

Then, I flipped to my easy cookbooks: the ones filled with quick pasta dishes, breading on everything, and gooey comfort food. Those recipes were definitely faster, but I knew I couldn't eat like that every night and feel great.

Why wasn't there anything in between? Something that was healthy, but also easy. Something that was delicious, but also nonintimidating after a long day. Something you could make on a normal weeknight with the things you had on hand. That would be my kind of cooking. There *had* to be a better way.

I started to experiment a bit: I'd squint at the complicated healthy recipes and try to guess what the basic essentials would be to keep all of the flavor and goodness, but with fewer ingredients and steps. I'd look at those quick comfort food recipes, and begin upgrading the ingredients, taking away the flour, extra sugars, or processed ingredients.

Incredibly, it started to work. Soon, I was making up my own creations, ones that fit my life with a full-time job and busy schedule: usually with five real-food ingredients or less, and in 15 minutes or less.

It became proof to me that you *could* have and do both things: eat healthy with less time and hassle. And that you didn't have to be a chef or expert cook to make it happen. In order to prove it and keep track of what I was doing each week, I started a blog. I retired my cookbooks into storage, and finally started to feel more confident in the kitchen: I began to realize that with anything I wanted to have, there was a way to make it real-food style. And usually very simply.

No more deprivation. No more trying to be perfect. No more hours wasted.

I started sharing the recipes and more about this little secret that I'd discovered: that real food was better, more delicious and easier than all the diets, all the marketing, and everything we've all been taught about being healthy. That eating and living this way gives you time back. It gives you better tasting, more beautiful food. And it gives you a steadier and more long-term way to be healthy, without being extreme, rigid, or always on a diet. And most of all, it was so much simpler, and such a happier way to eat and live.

Week by week, more and more people started following that little blog. I soon became obsessed with wanting to teach others about this way of living: if more people knew this, it could change their life, their perspective, their health, the amount of stress and anxiety they experienced, their energy for life, and their close relationships, too.

I continued cooking, blogging, and ended up going back to school to get a degree in nutrition and health coaching. In 2012, that little blog officially turned into what it is now: Simply Real Health, a full-service nutrition coaching and consulting company. And through the years, my mission and message have stayed the same: To help as many people as I can, eat real food, keep it simple, and live a more beautiful, intentional, and healthy life because of it. That it's not just the food that matters, it's how it affects your whole life. And the role it plays in every part of our lives.

THE PROBLEM

Unfortunately, my journey with food isn't a unique one. It's almost impossible to look at social media, listen to a podcast, or read a magazine these days without being bombarded with conflicting and ever-changing information on what to eat and not eat.

And, I mean, let's just admit it. We've probably all tried something, at some point: going Paleo or strictly vegan, drinking only juice or eating only butter for weeks at a time. We've signed up for that 3-day cleanse or 30-day challenge, so determined—once and for all, to get healthy, for good. We'll change our whole lives to make it work, declining all social invitations, meal prepping for hours each week, and running on fumes of willpower and determination alone.

But the problem? Real life is rarely perfect. And while a lot of these tactics might work in the short term, for a day or a few weeks at most, most of them don't last. They can't.

Because between work, family, friends, social commitments, traveling, changes in the seasons, and changes in our own personal seasons of life, those rigid rules are more than just unrealistic to keep up over time: they can suck the joy out of some of the most beautiful parts of life, too.

Because life without those salty, crunchy chips and guac, cold ice cream on a hot day, or rosé on girls' night? Yeah. It just ain't worth living. It's as though we think that if we can't do it all perfectly, then what's the point in trying?

As I did for most of my life, we swing back and forth, to one extreme or the other: being healthy and all in, or totally off the wagon, eating and drinking whatever we want, until we feel bad or guilty enough to start the cycle all over again. Most of us are all over the map trying to be healthier, living somewhere in between perfection, guilt, and deprivation, often all within the same week.

IT'S TIME FOR A BETTER WAY

A more simple way. A more intentional way. A more delicious way. And a more calm and joyful way to be healthy that can actually last for the rest of your life, with ease.

Without the extremes.

Without the guilt.

Without the information overload.

Without all the stress.

Because this much I know is true: it doesn't have to be so hard. We just have to make a change in how we're approaching it.

For most of us, this means that we have to wipe the slate totally clean. To forget all the old programming and outdated messages around food, and welcome in a new way of thinking about food that looks at our health in a much different and bigger picture way:

That it's not just about the food. It's about how deeply connected it is to the rest of our lives: physically, mentally, relationally, and emotionally, too. It's about learning how to live better in between the black and white rules, in the beautiful land of gray, as I like to call it: with more ease, more freedom, more simplicity, and more grace. In learning to embrace this, we can learn how to create a healthy lifestyle that actually lasts for our whole life.

Why does that matter? So we can take back our time and energy to focus on what really matters in life: the people we love, our purpose and work in this world, and to be the best version of ourselves as possible. Because we're only given a short time on this earth, so we might as well make it count.

So, welcome, my friend. To this way of life that I hope will simplify, encourage, and uplift you, as you go about your daily life, no matter how busy you are, or the season of life you are in.

GETTING STARTED

This book is my personal collection of the habits, foods, and recipes that have brought me back to good, over and over again, and the rituals behind them that have made a healthy lifestyle a lot more effortless, easy, and long-lasting.

Learning how to honor and weave in these little daily acts of kindness for my body over time has nourished, sustained, and filled me up physically, mentally, and emotionally, through many seasons in my own life.

I wrote this book in the hope that these ideas will do the same for you. I wrote this book because being healthy includes, but is so much more than, just the food you eat. To remind you that we always have a choice in our mood, our energy, and what we give to the world, starting with what we put in our mouth and on our table. It's all connected, always.

So, whether you're an entrepreneur, a leader, a parent or spouse, a student or seeker on a quest for your very best life, the equation is simple: eat real food most of the time, and you'll feel better. Do it daily and with intention and you will be unstoppable.

The ultimate goal? That you feel calm, empowered, and joyful around food, and in taking care of yourself, too. To find the joy in eating and being well, as a lifestyle that can last. Because we all need new ideas. Ways to stay inspired and ways to remind ourselves to keep things simple and create more joy in our lives. And a way to always have those options and ideas at our fingertips in the moments that we need them most.

This book that you hold in your hands is just that. It isn't just a cookbook.

It's a life book.

7 STEPS TO CREATING A HEALTHY LIFESTYLE THAT LASTS

1. The Mind-Set Reset
2. Eat Real Food
3. Clear the Clutter
4. Get Out of Autopilot
5. Bring the Joy
6. Define Your Nonnegotiables
7. Create Rituals

1. THE MIND-SET RESET

The best news of all is that the only thing you'll need to get started with this much more freeing and healthy way to live, is one very simple thing: a willingness to change how you're thinking about food. That instead of its being:

A chore.

A hassle.

The last thing on your to-do list.

The last thing you squeeze in sometimes, if you have time.

That your food—including the acts of buying it, cooking it, prepping it, ordering it, and eating it—is instead a radical and daily act of self-care, that you *get* to do and have a say in, every day.

Because, can I tell you a secret? Food is a profound source of power in your life, if you learn how to harness it well. It's where everything magical starts: with your mind-set and inner dialogue first. There are so many parts of life that we can't control, but our daily energy, how we think, our mood, how we treat others, how our body feels, all starts with what we put in our mouth each day.

So, my advice? Take back your ownership and power of this part of your life. If you feel like you don't have the time, make some room by clearing out some things or commitments in your life that aren't nourishing you back. Right here and right now, I'm giving you permission to do so. Because you are worth it. And your life is worth it. It's that big, and that important. And a required part of the work, if you want to live your best life.

2. EAT REAL FOOD

The next step in creating a healthy lifestyle that lasts? Wiping the slate clean and totally starting over with your definition of healthy food, as I did after those magical Italian days. To finally have the freedom to forget about those old-school and outdated rules, and 98 percent of what you think you already know. And instead: learn the difference between diet food that's marketed to us as healthy, and true, real food.

So, what exactly *is* the difference?

Real food is this: food in its most natural state. It's simple, natural, and has existed for thousands of years in relatively the same forms as we have today. They're often one-word foods, or have labels that list five or six ingredients that even an eight-year-old could pronounce.

What's *not* real food? Pretty much everything else. It's processed food, diet food, even most "health food." It's the food that is packaged to appear healthy on the front of the label, but when you look at the actual ingredients list, it has words you can't pronounce, or would take you a full five minutes to read.

So, take a peek right now in your desk, your car console, your purse, and especially your fridge or your pantry. Find some of your "healthy" food and take a second look. Is what you're eating made with a few real and simple ingredients? If not, upgrade it to something that is.

Because here's the truth, behind it all: if you can't pronounce it, your body can't, either. Keeping it simple and pure is kinder on your body. It really is as easy as that.

And the best part? Once you start looking at food like this, there are so many amazing and delicious options, most of which would be considered off limits for most diets: think of a life that now can happily include butter, real ice cream, whole milk, wine, potatoes, dark chocolate, well-sourced meat, and homemade baked goods. The result? A more simple, clear, and freeing perspective on food that will never change with the fads or seasons. Hallelujah.

3. CLEAR THE CLUTTER

Changing your mind-set and eating all real food are the first steps to a healthier and happier life, for sure. They are the unshakeable foundation. But it's the next piece that matters just as much if you want to create a healthy lifestyle that lasts: it's learning how to let go of the rest.

In other words, contrary to everything we've been taught, being healthy isn't about adding more things to think about in our day. Instead, it's about learning how to release the clutter that can keep us stuck in the same routines and habits for years on end. Clutter food. Clutter behaviors. Clutter routines. Clutter thoughts. Clutter emotions. Or even, clutter people.

This much I know is true: simplifying your food simplifies your life.

Even after just a week of eating real food, this step starts to happen naturally. Without all the chemicals, additives, and processed foods, your body immediately goes to work, detoxing, healing, and flooding every major system with the nutrient-dense food you're eating. All of your internal systems begin to normalize, optimize, and function so much better.

The result? Most people report having so much more energy, less brain fog, better quality sleep, easier digestion, fewer cravings, fewer ups and downs throughout the day, better mood, more patience, and more vibrancy in their daily lives. Over time, the result of this is so much bigger: a sense of calmness, clarity, and simplicity around food and the rest of your life starts to trickle in. And with it, a lot more space and freedom in your life for what actually matters and what, where, and who you want to spend your time with.

4. GET OUT OF AUTOPILOT

Eating real food, does more than simplify your life—it forces you out of autopilot, and gives you the space to actually start tuning *in* and listening to your body and the signals it's giving you, instead of tuning out. This concept is actually why most diets never work for the long term: because by nature, diets and set programs encourage you to tune out of your own body and mindlessly follow a set of predetermined rules.

But the real game changer is when you understand how *your* body operates best—in every occasion and situation. The types of food. The timing of your meals. The things that make you feel energized, and the things that don't.

All bodies do better on real food because that's how our system was designed, but every person is a little bit different and needs different things to feel his or her absolute best. So, part of this process is learning how to tune into your *own* body, listen to it, and trust the wisdom of what it's saying. It will rarely lead you astray.

You take your body wherever you go. So, get to know it. Learning how to read your body and rely

on the messages it's giving you is one of the biggest gifts you could ever give yourself.

5. BRING THE JOY

Tuning in to your body also finally allows the space for the best and most beautiful shift to take place: the ability to have more joy and enjoyment with food. Because a big part of having a healthy life is about actually enjoying it.

That it's not just about the food, but having a good relationship to it and to everything it's connected to. To be fully wherever you are. That instead of deprivation or perfection, you now have so much more room for the things, experiences, and foods you love most in life: great cocktails, cheese boards, great bread, eating out, and sharing meals with family and friends—all are an encouraged and celebrated part of living this kind of lifestyle.

But the key? Pick and stick to what you love. What foods do you truly love and enjoy and savor every bite or sip of? Which ones make life worth living? Define what they are for you, and get specific on what you love about them. Is it the taste, the texture, the temperature, or the ambience it comes with? Is it the first sip of a perfectly made handcrafted cocktail? Warm chocolate chip cookies, right out of the oven? Your best girlfriends sitting around a plate of gooey cheese and crackers? A juicy burger on date night? Find what's worth it for you, and then let go of the rest.

As long as they're chosen with intention and joy, there is plenty of room for these things to be sprinkled into your life.

6. DEFINE YOUR NONNEGOTIABLES

Something that most people don't realize is that designing a healthy life doesn't just happen naturally. We have to take an intentional and active role in creating it for ourselves.

And to do that, you have to have a deeper *why*.

An understanding of why being healthy is important to you. Because if you're just doing it to fit into a certain jeans size or see a specific number on a scale, that motivation fades pretty quickly. But having a deeper reason makes it about something so much more important: showing up for yourself, every single day.

I know that what I eat daily has a direct and immediate impact on how I feel mentally, physically, and emotionally. All of which impact how I show up, in all areas of my life: for myself, my business, and my relationships.

As humans, we don't do well with too much freedom or too much structure. We need a balance of both: a flexible framework that we can carry with us wherever we go, and something to lean into when life gets busy so we don't have to think so hard. This is where creating and defining your nonnegotiables begins.

"What are nonnegotiables?" you ask. They are small daily acts of self-care that have a high impact. They are two or three very simple actions that we can commit to doing daily that help keep us grounded, focused on what matters for our body, and accountable, no matter how busy our days or weeks get. Part of this is figuring out which behaviors and habits help encourage other healthy ones in your life. Think of them as the dominoes in your life.

Eating real food most of the time is one that everyone can (and, might I suggest, should) start with as a baseline. Committing to just this one act alone can change your life in such big and meaningful ways. Some other examples of non-negotiables could include: eating veggies every single day, or at every meal. Moving your body. Eating an actual lunch. Getting fresh air daily. Drinking enough water daily.

Think about the things that make the biggest difference for how *you* feel. Take note of them. Write them down. Commit to and honor them daily and watch them lead and guide you to such a better place. And if you need help, this book is full of fun ideas to get you started.

7. CREATE RITUALS

Once you have your nonnegotiables down, the next and final piece to creating a lifestyle you love is to take those two or three actions and make them a daily part of your life, in ways you enjoy and look forward to each day.

I call these your daily rituals. But don't worry. They don't require weird chanting or lighting a million tea lights.

A ritual is simply the art of taking care of ourselves—with joy.

Because one thing is for sure: life will always be busy, and it's easy to get distracted and pulled off track, even if we "know" what to do. We're human. So, the longer-lasting solution? We all need reminders built in to our days that help keep us accountable to how we want to live and feel.

Rituals are exactly that: tiny little acts, done with love daily, that add up over time and help you show up as your best self, each day. They can be different for everyone, but their message is the same: to help you pause, slow down, tune in, come back to the good, and ultimately, help you learn how to find the joy in taking care of yourself well.

The equation is easy to me: if I eat well and take care of myself, I feel good. And if I feel good, I do good. Because of this, eating real food and taking care of myself are high priorities in my life. They are nonnegotiables in my day that I make the time and space for first, as a commitment to myself.

ABOUT THIS BOOK

Simply Real Eating is a healthy lifestyle guidebook, organized by how our days and weeks actually play out, according to the time of day that you would actually use each recipe. Within each chapter, you'll also find inspiring ideas on how these recipes turn into your own healthy rituals throughout your days, weeks, and seasons, to help you create a healthy lifestyle that lasts. All with more simplicity and joy, and in ways that work in the midst of a busy life.

So, imagine:

Mornings sipping vibrant superfood lattes or smoothies, bites of better-than-coffee-shop baked healthy treats, warm cozy bowls, and satisfying weekend brunches.

Afternoons of easy make-ahead dishes, salads, and bowls for #lunchladies on the go; the realistic recipes you need to make your weekdays work with ease, no matter what else is going on.

When that late afternoon hunger pang hits? Your inspired snack game is covered.

Your healthier happy hours, done.

Evenings filled with beautiful and simple meals to help you gather around the table with the people you love the most, for both weeknight magic and hosting with ease. Your date nights, upgraded.

And, of course, guilt-free sweets and sips for every season and reason.

The recipes in this book are:

- Simple
- Easy
- Naturally gluten-free and food sensitivity–friendly
- All real food
- Often five ingredients or fewer (not including staples, such as olive oil, salt, and pepper)—or close to it
- Delicious

Before we jump in, I want you to know that whether you are a seasoned cook or a total beginner in the kitchen, a real-food veteran, or someone who's just beginning his or her own health journey, my wish for you is this:

That you take this book, these recipes, and these rituals and weave them into your daily life and kitchen, at whatever pace works for you.

That you release any pressure or perfectionist tendencies on trying to do this real-food cooking thing, perfectly.

That you get in there, and get messy. Try new things. Write in the margins. Create, play, and give yourself grace to laugh at yourself and to have fun with this process, and not take it too seriously. I am not a trained chef. I *still* have terrible knife skills, and a hard time following the rules, so if I can do it, you can, too.

That you make the space for good food, and the time for it to work some extra magic in your life, because it always will if you let it.

That you start to see that baby steps and small daily actions are what add up over time for an exceptional, happier and healthier life, and that what you're doing (and eating) most of the time is what matters more than any drastic short-term fix.

That you take it one day at a time, one meal at a time, and one tiny decision at a time.

That you just start to incorporate more real food into your life.

That with it, you find your own land of gray: with more joy, more health, and more love of good food. All made simple.

RITUAL #1: SIMPLIFY YOUR WEEK

THE RITUAL: Carve out 15 minutes before the week starts to take an inventory of what's coming up.

1. Make it sacred: Show up as if it's a real appointment; this time and consistency matters if you want to live a healthy lifestyle that lasts throughout all the days, weeks, and seasons of your life.

2. Remember your nonnegotiables: Is any prep needed to make them happen every day? Do you need to prefill your water bottles, prep some veggies, throw something in the slow cooker, or carve out time for a moment of self-care?

3. Make plans to shop: Online, at the store, at your local farmers' market, the way you do it doesn't matter; the point is that you take some time to surround yourself with good food for the week.

If you're not the structured meal-planning type, ask yourself these questions:

1. What do you need a little more of this week? And what do you need a little less of? Start with food. Bonus points for including other things, such as self-care, sleep, social commitments, and where you're spending your free time.

2. How many nights will you most likely be eating in? How many nights will you be eating out? Pick one to three recipes to make.

3. What's your lunch situation? Pick one or two make-ahead, one-pot, or #lunchlady recipes. If you are eating out, pick what restaurant you might be at and what you will likely get. Doing this work ahead of time can save you from so many subpar last-minute decisions.

4. Are there any potential obstacles that might get in the way of being your healthiest self this week?

SETTING UP, PANTRY MEALS, AND MEAL PLANNING

THE ART OF EASIER WEEKLY MEAL PLANNING: MY FLEXIBLE BLUEPRINT, DECODED!

Confession: I am so not a meal planner. I prefer and actually enjoy figuring out my food each day, based on what my body needs that week, the time of year, the weather, and so on. But because having *no* plan doesn't work, and being overly planned makes me feel too confined, this is my living-in-the-land-of-gray solution: I like to have good things ready in my fridge, and a well-stocked pantry every week.

These are nonnegotiables for me.

So, every week, I buy a few basic and very versatile ingredients that can be used in at least two ways. This is my version of a flexible framework: it helps me be intentional and prepared, but with plenty of freedom and flexibility to modify or change things up.

The following list is a roundup of my favorite staple meals to help you make healthy eating more doable, easy, and inspiring any night of the week. This is based on feeding two adults and one little one who are mostly eating at home each week. Feel free to adjust, based on what your own needs are.

A one-pot meal (1 per week): A veggie-based meal made with or without broth or sauce that you can add toppings, meat, or beans to as the week progresses:

- **Soup**, such as 3-Ingredient Tomato Soup (page 131), Healthy Veggie Noodle Pho (page 132), Roasted Kabocha Squash Soup (page 135), or Cozy Roasted Parsnip Soup (page 129)
- **Make-ahead salad**, such as The Real Greek Salad (page 100), Herby Roasted Corn Salad (page 213), Pesto Quinoa and Tomato Salad (page 106), or Roasted Cauliflower, Carrot, and Tahini Salad (page 120)
- **Skillet sauté**, such as The Warm Shaved Brussels Sprout Caesar (page 171), Crustless Chicken Sausage and Veggie Pizza (page 167), Broccoli Rice Paella (page 180)
- **Slow cooker recipe**, such as The Italian Situation (page 199) or Sweet Potato Turkey Chili (page 200)

Protein (1 to 2 per week): Substances you can add to any meals, which have under 10 minutes of prep:

- **Roasted organic chicken**, for soups, salads, tacos, bowls, and skillet sautés
- **Organic ground turkey, chicken, or lamb**, for burgers, meatballs, skillet sautés, meat loaf, tacos, and salads
- **Nitrate-free organic turkey slices**, for salads, bowls, open-faced sandwiches, and snacks
- **Wild fish or seafood (fresh or frozen)**, to grill, bake, roast, skillet sauté, and add to salads or stews
- **Wild smoked salmon**, for salads, bowls, eggs, and meze plates
- **Wild tuna or sardines (canned)**, for salads, make-ahead salads, bowls, open-faced sandwiches, or to grill
- **Pastured organic eggs**, for salads, deli-style salads, scrambles, baking, or hard-boiling

Dressing or sauce (1 per week): For salads, roasted veggies, or potatoes; mixed into quinoa; as a marinade for meat; or for other make-ahead dishes for the week:

- Hummus (page 155)
- Pesto (page 106)
- Salad dressings or sauces (see *The Simply Real Health Cookbook* and blog for even more dressing and sauce recipes)

Vegetables (2 to 4 per week): For roasting, adding to soups, salads, stews, sautés, or grilling. The most versatile veggies are:

- Broccoli
- Carrots
- Cauliflower
- Celery

- Cucumbers
- Red peppers
- Tomatoes
- Zucchini

Greens (1 to 2 per week): For smoothies, skillet sautés, lettuce wraps and salad bases, or topping soups and stews. The most versatile greens are:

- Arugula
- Butter lettuce
- Chard

- Kale
- Romaine lettuce
- Spinach

THE 12 CATEGORIES OF REAL FOOD

Real foods are simple, pure, and whole. There are 12 basic categories:

Vegetables	Meat
Fruit	Eggs
Nuts and seeds	Dairy
Beans and legumes	Grains
Seafood	Healthy fats
Poultry	Natural sweeteners

What is not real food?

Pretty much everything else

Starches and grains (1 to 2 each week): As substantial feeling sides to add as you'd like:

- Brown rice pasta
- Buckwheat
- Corn (tortillas, on the cob, corn chips, polenta, etc.)
- Millet
- Potatoes

- Quinoa
- Rice
- Squash (butternut, spaghetti, delicata, kabocha, etc.)
- Sweet potatoes/yams

Healthy fats (1 to 2 each week): To add as toppings to salads, in smoothies, soups, bowls, and skillet sautés:

- Avocado
- Cheeses, such as Parmesan, feta, goat cheese (organic)
- Coconut milk (canned)

- Garlic olive oil
- Hemp, chia, sunflower, or pumpkin seeds
- Nuts or nut butters

A NOTE ABOUT GLUTEN AND DAIRY

Something that you may (or may not) have noticed about this book is that every recipe is what I call naturally gluten-free. Meaning that instead of relying on gluten substitutes or processed health food, all the ingredients in this book are naturally occurring. As someone who has been gluten-free for over a decade (for health reasons that I talk about on the blog), I think gluten is something everyone can be just a little more mindful of their consumption of, no matter whether their body reacts to it physically (this can range from stomach and digestive issues to skin issues to chronic pain to brain fog and sleeplessness and so much in between). Wheat has become one of the most inflammatory foods in our society because of modern processing techniques, so having recipes that leave it out naturally is a great move to make for the food you eat regularly. But as always, I encourage you to do what's best for your body and for those you are cooking for. If that means pairing a soup with a freshly baked baguette or crafting up one of the pizza recipes and using homemade three-ingredient dough for a special occasion, do it. Just choose simple high-quality ingredients that your body can digest.

Dairy can be similarly problematic and is something to be mindful of, in terms of the quality, types, and frequency that your body does best with. For most people, just starting by upgrading the quality and sourcing of your dairy to the most pure and unprocessed forms is all that's needed (a.k.a., going organic when you can, staying away from added hormones and pesticides, and sticking with less-processed, whole-milk versions). Every person's body is different in what they tolerate, but, for most people, butter and small amounts of Parmesan, feta, or goat cheeses are the most easily digestible (and therefore are the ones I include most often in this book). If you can't tolerate any dairy products well, feel free to leave it out of the recipe completely, or use easy substitutions like coconut milk yogurt, nut milk, and so forth.

STAPLES

Here's my full list of staples for a well-stocked fridge and pantry—my key to making healthy meals on the fly. (Visit the Simply Real Health website for a list of my favorite brands.)

Your Weekly Fridge and Produce Roundup

The 15 most versatile fridge staples and groceries to have on hand:

Avocados

Bananas

Basil (optional, for homemade dressing, pesto, sauces, and garnishes)

Carrots

Celery

Garlic

Large organic, cage-free eggs

Leafy greens (kale, spinach, arugula, romaine lettuce, butter lettuce)

Lemons (or red wine vinegar or cider vinegar in your pantry)

Meat or protein of your choice

Olives

Onions

Organic grass-fed butter

Parmesan

Peppers

Potatoes, sweet potatoes, or winter squash

Sauerkraut, pickles, or pickled veggies

Veggies of your choice (2 or 3)

Whole-milk Greek yogurt or coconut yogurt

Whole or nondairy milk

Your Freezer Roundup

The 9 most versatile freezer staples to always have on hand:

Brown rice pizza crust

Burgers (clean veggie or organic, grass-fed meat)

Chicken breasts (organic)

Fish (wild)

Green frozen veggies of your choice (broccoli, green beans, etc.)

Sauces (homemade)

Sausage (ground and links, nitrate-free)

Shrimp (wild)

Smoothie ingredients (bananas, blueberries, kale/spinach, avocado pieces, etc.)

Your Pantry Roundup

My building-block pantry staples:

Basic Everyday Pantry Staples

Beans (a variety, canned or dried)

Brown rice noodles

Canned pumpkin

Canned soups

Canned tomatoes, tomato paste, and jarred tomato sauce

Coconut butter

Coconut milk

Curry paste

Dark chocolate (it's not just for baking!)

Dried fruit (a variety)

Garbanzo bean flour

Ghee
Gluten-free crackers
Jarred green salsa
Lentils
Miso powder/paste
Nut butter
Nuts (a variety)
Polenta
Quinoa

Pantry Staples for Baking

Almond meal
Avocado oil
Baking powder
Baking soda
Balsamic vinegar
Blackstrap molasses
Chocolate chips
Cider vinegar
Coconut flakes
Coconut flour
Coconut oil

Spices

Chili powder
Cinnamon
Cumin
Herbes de Provence
Nutmeg
Pepper
Red pepper flakes
Sea salt

Rice
Roasted red peppers
Sardines
Seeds (chia, pumpkin, sesame, etc.)
Stock (chicken or vegetable, organic)
Sun-dried tomatoes
Tortillas, organic corn
Tuna

Gluten-free flour blend
Gluten-free rolled and steel-cut oats
Honey
Olive oil
Organic cane sugar
Pure maple syrup
Pure vanilla extract
Red wine vinegar
Tamari
Toasted sesame oil

Truth: You have to eat every day, so don't let it catch you by surprise.

THE ART OF PANTRY MEALS

These five delicious meals can be quickly thrown together with your staples. No shopping or planning ahead required.

Curry paste + coconut milk + veggies/meat/beans = **Curry**

Veggies and/or meat + rice + greens + parmesan cheese = **Risotto**

Chicken breasts + mild green salsa = **Chicken Verde**

Lentils + veggies + broth + onion + garlic = **Lentil Soup**

Ground meat/steak/chicken/shrimp/veggies + peppers + avocado + corn tortillas = **Tacos**

MORNING
MAGIC

BEVVIE LADY 101

Power-Up Cups and Superfood Lattes
to Get the Day Started Right

Sarah's Matcha Latte   31

Vanilla Cold Brew   32

Healthy Pumpkin Spice Latte   35

Maca Hot Chocolate   36

Golden Milk Turmeric Latte   39

Earl Grey Cinnamon Latte   40

Homemade Nut Milk   42

Get your day started right. It's a message most of us grew up with. But let's be honest: in real life, mornings are often the busiest time of day, and therefore the easiest time to fall into robotic autopilot habits—gulping coffee to wake up, quickly spooning down a bowl of cereal, or wrapping a piece of toast in a paper towel and running out the door.

A better solution? To create a more stable and grounded start to our day, one that's relatively quick and easy to do (because you're probably doing it already in some capacity). Introducing what I call the Morning Bevvie.

RITUAL #2: SET YOUR INTENTIONS

THE RITUAL: Check in to remind yourself of what you want to focus your energy on and what you want to call into your day. Setting your intentions and energy in the beginning of your day can help minimize distractions or actions that don't line up with how you ultimately want to feel and perform in all of your day. The best part: all you need is five minutes.

Think about or jot down these things:

1. **Your top three most important tasks to get done that day.** Make another list of "if you have time" tasks.
2. **What's your lunch plan that day?**
3. **What's your dinner plan that day?**
4. **Any other nonnegotiable habits/reminders that you need that day?**

RITUAL #3: UPGRADE YOUR BEVVIE

THE RITUAL: Start every morning with an upgraded bevvie.
The formula: water + base bevvie + cream element + sweetener + optional add-ins of your choice

1. **Pick your temperature:** hot or iced water.
2. **Choose a base bevvie that works well for your body:** herbal tea, green or black tea, yerba maté, matcha, coffee, or cold brew.
3. **Choose a cream component that works well for your body:** heavy whipping cream, half-and-half, milk, butter, ghee, coconut butter, coconut oil, collagen peptide powder, or homemade nut milk.
4. **Choose a sweetener that works well for your body, if any:** coconut water, a splash of vanilla extract, pure maple syrup, or honey.
5. **Blend together or stir.**
6. **Pour into a beautiful mug or glass that brings you joy.**

Bevvie Closet Essentials

Adaptogenic mushroom powder (chaga, lion's mane, rhodiola, reishi)
Butter (organic, grass-fed)
Cinnamon
Cocoa powder (unsweetened)

Coconut butter
Coconut oil
Coconut sugar
Collagen peptide powder
Ghee
Honey

Maple syrup (pure)
Matcha (organic)
MCT oil
Vanilla extract

Sarah's Matcha Latte

Makes 1 serving

Matcha is a powdered green tea that has some truly magical properties. If you follow my blog, you know that matcha is my number one go-to drink: it's energizing like coffee, without the crash afterward. As you get into matcha, start with ½ teaspoon of the powder, and work your way up to 1 teaspoon. I use half water and half almond milk, but you can use all milk if you like it creamier, or try adding 1 teaspoon of coconut butter, coconut oil, grass-fed butter, or a combination to blend. You can also add cinnamon, collagen peptides, or other adaptogenic powders of your choice (see page 30). Beautiful served hot or cold.

½ cup Homemade Nut Milk
(page 42) or milk of your
choice

½ teaspoon matcha powder

½ teaspoon pure maple syrup
or honey (optional)

Pour ½ cup of water and nut milk into a sauce-pan over medium heat and bring to a simmer. Place the matcha powder in a blender and pour the hot milk mixture in, adding your choice of sweetener, if using, and any other additions. Blend on high speed for 20 seconds before serving.

Have an extra minute or two? Make a quick list of things you're grateful for. By calling more attention to all the good in your life, you magnetically create more of it.

Vanilla Cold Brew

Makes 2 servings

As far as coffee goes, cold brew is one of the healthiest and best forms you can drink, because its acid content is so much lower than regular brewed versions. For that reason, a lot of people can tolerate it better. But it does have quite the caffeine kick, so keep that in mind—you might need less than normal for superpowered results. The best part? You can easily make it at home, if you make it ahead of time. And it's just as good heated up for homemade lattes and cold-weather bevvies. You can also add a dash of honey or maple syrup, if desired, or a few sticks of cinnamon as the coffee chills.

¼ cup organic coffee beans

1 vanilla bean (in the pod),
or 1 teaspoon pure vanilla extract

1 teaspoon pure maple syrup
or honey (optional)

Grind the coffee beans. Bring 1½ to 2 cups of water to a boil in a saucepan or kettle.

Split open the vanilla bean pod and scrape the seeds into a French press coffeemaker. Add the ground coffee and pour the hot water over it. Add your choice of sweetener, if desired, and stir well. Cover and refridgerate for at least 12 hours, and up to 24, before straining and pouring out the liquid into a glass mason jar for storage.

Pour the cold brew over ice and add your favorite milk or coconut water.

Healthy Pumpkin Spice Latte

Makes 1 serving

That's right, the real deal. Your favorite fall bevvie, with all the joy and none of the chemies. You can make this latte with coffee, Vanilla Cold Brew (page 32), espresso, or tea. Also optional is to add adaptogens, collagen peptides, or coconut butter.

"What to do with the rest of the pumpkin?" you ask. Make a batch of Mini Pumpkin Spice Doughnuts (page 75), use it in place of squash in Butternut Squash and Cardamom Pancakes (page 84), or in place of sweet potato in Sweet Potato Morning Muffins (page 70).

¼ cup pure pumpkin puree

1 tablespoon pure maple syrup or honey, or to taste

1 teaspoon pumpkin pie spice, plus more for serving

½ teaspoon pure vanilla extract

Coffee, Earl Grey or rooibos tea brewed in ½ cup water, or 2 shots of espresso,

Homemade Nut Milk (page 42), milk of your choice, or coconut water

Ground cinnamon or freshly grated nutmeg, for serving (optional)

Combine the pumpkin puree, maple syrup, pumpkin pie spice, and vanilla in a small saucepan. Heat over low heat and whisk the ingredients together. Add the brewed coffee or tea, then the milk of your choice. Transfer to a blender and blend on high speed for at least 20 seconds to get a beautiful froth. Pour into a mug and sprinkle with extra pumpkin pie spice, cinnamon, or nutmeg to serve.

Maca Hot Chocolate

Makes 1 serving

Maca is an amazing superfood powder, known for its ability to naturally balance your hormones, give you amazing energy, and boost your mood. On its own, the taste can be a bit bitter, but when blended with chocolate and warming spices, the result is delicious. Using a milk of your choice here, instead of water, produces a creamier result (or blend with ½ teaspoon of coconut oil, coconut butter, or a scoop of collagen peptide powder). Skip the maca completely to make an amazing homemade hot chocolate, or try the Date Hot Chocolate that follows.

1 cup Homemade Nut Milk (page 42), milk of your choice, or water

1 teaspoon maca powder

1 teaspoon unsweetened cocoa powder, plus more to garnish

1 teaspoon ground cinnamon, plus more to garnish

1 teaspoon pure vanilla extract

½ to 1 teaspoon pure maple syrup (optional)

Bring the milk or water to a boil in a saucepan or kettle. Combine the maca powder, cocoa powder, cinnamon, vanilla, and maple syrup, if using, in a blender. Pour in the hot liquid and blend well. Pour into your favorite mug and sprinkle with cocoa powder and cinnamon to serve.

Variation
Date Hot Chocolate

Add **½ cup nut milk, ½ cup water, 1 ½ teaspoons unsweetened cocoa powder, 2 pitted dates,** and **1 teaspoon vanilla** to a saucepan and bring to a simmer. When hot, pour the liquid into a blender and blend until smooth, about 1 minute. Add a dash of maple syrup, cinnamon, and/or butter as you blend, if you desire.

Golden Milk Turmeric Latte

Makes 1 serving

Golden milk is a traditional Ayurvedic drink made with turmeric, ginger, and spices and is used for healing of all kinds: for your immune system and nervous system especially. Turmeric is a natural anti-inflammatory and ginger soothes and eases upset stomachs; when they are combined with a healthy fat, such as coconut oil or butter, your body can most easily absorb all the nutrients. I love making the base for this latte—the Healing Golden Milk Paste that follows—every fall and winter and keeping a jar in the fridge, for easy access.

For the latte, add any of these optional ingredients if desired: a teaspoon of butter, ghee, collagen, or adaptogens of your choice. To serve iced, make the warm version first and let cool.

1 cup Homemade Nut Milk (page 42), milk of your choice, or water

1 teaspoon honey or pure maple syrup (optional)

1 teaspoon Healing Golden Milk Paste (recipe follows)

Heat the milk and sweetener, if using, in a small saucepan. Place the golden milk paste in a blender, pour in the hot liquid, and blend for at least 20 seconds for a beautiful froth. Serve hot.

Healing Golden Milk Paste

Makes 8 teaspoon-size servings

I like to leave my golden milk paste unsweetened so I can use it in both sweeter and savory things—add a teaspoon to warm veggies, curries, salad dressings, soups, or Golden Milk Pots of Gold (page 55). Be sure to use a stainless-steel saucepan and be careful with the turmeric—it can stain easily.

Add **2 ½ tablespoons ghee, butter, or coconut oil, ¼ cup ground turmeric, 2 to 3 teaspoons ground cinnamon, 1 to 2 teaspoons ground ginger, 1 teaspoon black pepper,** and **½ cup water** to a small saucepan over medium heat. Stir gently until the mixture forms a paste, adding more water if it thickens too quickly. Transfer your golden milk paste to a glass jar with a lid to store in the fridge for up to four weeks.

Earl Grey Cinnamon Latte

Makes 1 serving

Trying to let up a little on the caffeine intake? Whether it's in place of your usual coffee or as a less intense afternoon boost, this tea-based latte is a perfect one to have in your arsenal. You can make this version with rooibos, chamomile, or chocolate tea, too.

2 Earl Grey tea bags,
    or 2 teaspoons loose tea
½ cup milk of your choice
    or coconut water
1 teaspoon pure maple syrup
    or honey
1 to 2 teaspoons coconut butter
½ teaspoon ground cinnamon,
    plus more for serving

Brew the tea in ½ cup water.

In a separate saucepan, heat the milk, maple syrup, coconut butter, and cinnamon together. Then, add the warm tea. Transfer to a blender and blend on high speed for at least 20 seconds to get a beautiful froth. Top with extra cinnamon to serve.

Homemade Nut Milk

Makes 8 to 10 servings

If you've ever read the ingredient label on most alternative milk, you know how rare it is to find ones that are actually clean—without the emulsifiers and chemicals. But, as it turns out, making your own at home is actually much easier than people think. I love making it a part of my Sunday routine, and mixing it up each week. Feel free to try this recipe with other nuts or seeds of your choice (such as cashews, hazelnuts, macadamia nuts, Brazil nuts, hemp seeds or pumpkin seeds, or even oats). Order a nut milk bag online to make this easy on yourself, or use a fine-mesh sieve to strain out the pulp.

4 cups almonds, or nuts or seeds
    of your choice
1 teaspoon cider vinegar or
    freshly squeezed lemon juice
1 tablespoon pure vanilla extract

Up to 48 hours before: Combine the almonds and enough water to cover them by at least an inch in a large glass or nonreactive metal bowl. Add 1 teaspoon cider vinegar or squeeze of lemon juice and soak for at least 24 hours, covered, on the counter or in the fridge.

When ready to make, drain and rinse the almonds well, then pour into a blender with 6 cups of fresh water and the vanilla. Blend on high speed until everything is liquefied. Pour the liquid through a nut milk bag or fine strainer, into a large glass bottle, bowl, or pitcher with a lid. Store in the fridge for up to 10 days.

RITUAL #4: WATER YOUR BODY

THE RITUAL: Start the morning with 16 ounces of water.

Why? Because more often then not, our body is more dehydrated than in need of immediate food in the morning.

Although it sounds so simple, drinking water as a steady practice in your life and throughout your day will help you regulate so many of the systems in your body that directly control how you feel each day: your digestion, your energy, your hunger, and your moods being the most common.

To try yourself: A good rule of thumb is to take your weight (in pounds) and divide that number by two. This is the approximate amount of ounces of water your body needs in a day to function best. Timing-wise, water as a ritual in your day could look something like this:

- At least 16 ounces before your morning bevvie and breakfast
- At least 16 to 32 ounces before lunch
- At least 32 to 40 ounces before dinner

Tips:

- Think you're hungry? Drink 16 ounces of water first. Hunger is often confused for your body's need for hydration.
- Try to be done with the majority of your water drinking by around 6 p.m., so that you're not up all night visiting the bathroom.
- Drink the bulk of your water away from your meals. Doing so helps prevent your diluting the natural digestive enzymes that help you digest and break down your food.
- Make it fun! Find a water bottle you love the feel of or that is easy for you to drink from; mix up the temperature; use a straw; add lemons, limes, oranges, berries, citrus, or bubbles.

WEEKDAY WORK IT

Easy and Make-Ahead Recipes for Busy Mornings

Everyday Smoothie Bowls   46

Chocolate Green Smoothies   49

Carrot, Turmeric, and Ginger Smoothie   50

The Busy Girl Smoothie   52

The Morning Warming Smoothie   53

Golden Milk Pots of Gold   55

Coconut, Coffee, and Cocoa Nib Overnight "Oats"   56

Cauliflower Rice Cups   58

Honey Butter and Oatmeal Breakfast Cookies   59

The Anytime Breakfast Bowl   61

Seasonal Jam Dots   62

Cranberry Walnut Grain-Free Granola   65

Savory Yogurt Bowls   66

Grain-Free Seedy Bread   69

Sweet Potato Morning Muffins   70

Breakfast. The so-called most important meal of the day, especially if you are trying to be healthy. But the real truth? Eating any of the typical breakfast foods in the morning (cereal, toast, baked goods, etc.), will probably make you more hungry and tired in the hours that follow it, than less.

My approach instead: after your morning water sesh and healthy bevvie, ask yourself first whether you are truly hungry. So many of us eat breakfast based purely on the principle that we "should," instead of checking in with ourselves first. As you eat more real and nutrient-dense food, you'll find that your hunger starts to decrease overall. You just don't need the same volume or frequency of food, as before. Yes, even at breakfast. Or shall I say, *especially* at breakfast.

But if the answer to your hunger question is in fact a yes, give any of these easy options a try. All will infuse your body with mega-nutrients, healthy fats, protein, vegetables, and magical real foods, which will help you take on the day in a much steadier way.

Everyday Smoothie Bowls

Makes 1 serving

While classic açai bowls are beautiful (and delicious), they're also usually very high in natural sugar, which can spike and crash your blood sugar within the hour. A little upgrade? These recipes take the same idea, but add some good healthy fats and protein to help keep you satisfied. The secret key to a fulfilling and thick smoothie bowl texture is using as little water and liquid as you can, and freezing the banana ahead of time.

For the Red Raspberry and Beet Smoothie Bowl I use leftover beets, which are packed with vitamin C, for a stunning color and immune system–boosting powers, and for the Green Kale Smoothie Bowl, I add a healthy boost of greens. Use whatever smoothie add-ins or toppings you like, but I love these combos.

RED RASPBERRY AND BEET SMOOTHIE BOWL

1 small cooked beet
½ cup raspberries
½ avocado
½ banana
1 tablespoon clean protein powder
    (see note on page 138)
1 cup ice cubes
Optional toppings: hemp seeds, chia seeds,
    coconut flakes, goji berries, raspberries,
    or sliced apple

GREEN KALE SMOOTHIE BOWL

2 to 3 stemmed kale leaves or 3 to 4 handfuls
    of spinach
½ avocado
½ banana
1 to 2 teaspoons nut butter
2 teaspoons chia seeds (optional)
1 tablespoon clean protein powder
    (see note on page 138)
1 cup ice cubes
Optional toppings: unsweetened cocoa nibs,
    chopped walnuts, large coconut flakes,
    mulberries, dried blueberries, or goji berries

Add all of the ingredients for your chosen smoothie bowl, except for the ice and toppings, to a blender with ¼ cup of water. Blend until smooth. Add the ice and continue to blend, adding small amounts of additional water if needed to blend. Scrape the smoothie into a serving bowl, using a spatula. Sprinkle with toppings of your choice to serve.

Chocolate Green Smoothies

Makes 1 serving

Because mint and chocolate together is never a bad idea. This may be the most guilt-free way to enjoy the two: in a green smoothie that will serve and lift you up in the hours that follow it. This smoothie is also great without the mint. For a version with a double boost of energy, try the Coffee Chocolate Green Buzz Smoothie.

**MINT CHOCOLATE
GREEN SMOOTHIE**

½ fresh or frozen banana

2 cups spinach

15 mint leaves

2 tablespoons cocoa nibs or 2 teaspoons
    unsweetened cocoa powder

½ medium zucchini, roughly chopped

2 pitted dates

1 scoop clean protein powder (optional; see note
    on page 138)

1 cup ice

Cinnamon or cocoa powder, for topping
    (optional)

**COFFEE CHOCOLATE
GREEN BUZZ SMOOTHIE**

1 cup cold brewed coffee

2 tablespoons cocoa nibs

1 frozen banana

3 cups spinach

¼ cup Homemade Nut Milk (page 42)
    or milk of your choice

1 cup ice

Cinnamon or cocoa powder, for topping
    (optional)

Add all of the ingredients for your chosen smoothie, except for the ice, to a blender. Blend until well combined. Add the ice and continue to blend until smooth. Serve cold, topped with cinnamon or cocoa powder, if desired.

NOTE: You can substitute stemmed kale leaves for the spinach in either recipe.

Carrot, Turmeric, and Ginger Smoothie

Makes 1 serving

Packed full of vitamin C, beta-carotene, and the immune and nervous system–healing properties of turmeric and ginger, this smoothie will start your day off right! To up the creaminess factor on this smoothie, add another half of a frozen banana or a splash of coconut milk.

1 carrot, chopped

1 small orange

½ banana, frozen

½ cup frozen or fresh cubed mango

½ cup coconut water

1½ teaspoons grated fresh turmeric, or ¼ teaspoon ground

1 teaspoon grated fresh ginger, or ¼ teaspoon ground

Pinch of cayenne pepper (optional)

1 tablespoon hulled hemp seeds or chia seeds (optional)

½ cup ice

Place all the ingredients, except the ice, in a blender and blend until well combined. Add the ice and continue to blend until smooth. Serve cold.

The Busy Girl Smoothie

Makes 1 serving

This is my go-to smoothie when things are busy and I need a quick and solid boost of energy that will hold me over well into the afternoon. This is also the combo that I order out at smoothie bars because the ingredients are so widely available.

½ banana
2 to 3 kale leaves, stemmed,
    or 2 cups spinach
½ cup almond or coconut milk
1 teaspoon spirulina powder
    (optional)
1 scoop collagen peptides or clean
    protein powder (optional)
½ cup ice

Place all the ingredients, except the ice, in a blender with ½ cup of water and blend until well combined. Add the ice and continue to blend until smooth.

The Morning Warming Smoothie

Makes 1 serving

In the winter, it's hard to get motivated to drink a cold smoothie. So, my little winter hack: I make this warming, no-sugar-added one instead! I love this smoothie heated up a bit, like a morning soup, but room temperature is also delicious. This recipe is so great for using up leftover veggies from the night before—I like to prep and cook all the ingredients in the evening to make it easy to make these smoothies all week. A little cinnamon or nutmeg makes a beautiful addition on top.

1 sweet potato, roasted and skin removed

½ medium zucchini, roasted or steamed

½ cup spinach

1 cup broccoli stems, roasted or steamed (see note)

½ cup Homeade Nut Milk (page 42) or milk of your choice

1 teaspoon ground cinnamon

¼ cup ice (optional)

Place all the ingredients, except the ice, in a blender and blend until smooth. Add the ice, if using, and blend again until smooth.

NOTE: This smoothie is a great way to use the stems from your broccoli, but you can use florets, too.

Golden Milk Pots of Gold

Makes 1 serving

This is a really good way to get some extra anti-inflammatory power in your day, and an easy snack or quick breakfast if you have the Healing Golden Milk Paste (page 39) in the fridge. Keeps well in the fridge for up to eight days.

1 cup coconut milk
¼ cup chia seeds
1 teaspoon Healing Golden Milk
    Paste (page 39)
Optional toppings: handful of
    cocoa nibs, coconut flakes,
    raisins, goji berries, sliced
    banana, or blueberries

Combine the coconut milk, chia seeds, and golden milk paste in a small glass mason jar with a lid. Shake well and then chill in the fridge for at least an hour for the mixture to solidify. Add whatever toppings you'd like when ready to eat.

Coconut, Coffee, and Cocoa Nib Overnight "Oats"

Makes 2 servings

This superfood breakfast is totally grain-free and full of great protein and healthy fats to keep you full and satisfied throughout the morning—and it's so easy to make ahead of time. Add gluten-free oats if you prefer a more traditional twist, or mix in fun toppings, such as chopped dates, coconut flakes, maca or matcha powder, or other nuts or seeds of your choice.

½ cup shelled hemp seeds

¼ cup brewed coffee (see note)

¼ cup Homemade Nut Milk (page 42) or milk of your choice

1 tablespoon shredded unsweetened coconut

4 teaspoons chia seeds

1 teaspoon pure maple syrup

1 teaspoon ground cinnamon

1 teaspoon cocoa nibs

Combine all the ingredients in a small glass jar and shake well. Chill in the fridge for at least 4 hours, or overnight. Serve warm or at room temperature, with toppings of your choice.

NOTE: For a version without coffee, use ½ cup nut milk.

Cauliflower Rice Cups

Makes 12 muffins

This is one of my favorite recipes to make ahead for busy weeks. They're also amazing made with broccoli rice as a base and different types of cheese (try crumbled goat or feta). Make a batch for the week, freeze, and warm them up when you're ready to eat.

Coconut oil spray (optional)

2 cups cauliflower rice

2 cups cooked broccoli florets, chopped

½ red bell pepper, seeded and diced

2 large organic, cage-free eggs

1 green onion, finely chopped

½ cup chopped fresh parsley, basil, spinach, or arugula

¼ cup plus 2 tablespoons brown rice flour, gluten-free oat flour, or gluten-free flour blend

1 tablespoon herbes de Provence

1 teaspoon sea salt

1 teaspoon freshly ground black pepper

½ cup grated Parmesan (optional)

Preheat the oven to 425°F and line a muffin tin with paper liners or spray with coconut oil.

Combine all the ingredients in a bowl and mix well. Fill the muffin cups halfway and bake for 24 to 27 minutes, until the tops are slightly browned.

Honey Butter and Oatmeal Breakfast Cookies

Makes 12 cookies

Who says cookies can't be a breakfast food? When made with the right powerhouse ingredients and just a tiny touch of natural sweetener, they are a great healthy option to make ahead for busy weeks. Store in an airtight container for up to one week. These are delicious smeared with natural nut butter, too.

5 tablespoons grass-fed butter,
    ghee, or coconut oil
2 tablespoons honey or pure
    maple syrup
1 cup almond meal
1 cup gluten-free rolled oats
2 tablespoons flaxseeds
1 tablespoon chia seeds
1 teaspoon pure vanilla extract
Pinch of sea salt

Preheat the oven to 375°F and line a baking sheet with parchment paper.

Warm the butter and honey in a small saucepan over low heat until they melt. Place the honey mixture plus all the remaining ingredients a small bowl and mix well to combine.

Form into 12 small cookie balls, place an inch apart on the prepared baking sheet, and flatten slightly with your finger. Bake for 18 to 20 minutes, until golden brown.

The Anytime Breakfast Bowl

Makes 2 servings

When most people think of breakfast, it's either eggs or something sweet and carbohydrate based. But the truth is this: if you're not hungry enough to eat vegetables—even in the morning— you're probably not really hungry at all. So, in my eyes, this is the perfect breakfast meal: it's warm and filling, vegetable forward, and also conveniently happens to make use of some common dinner leftovers. I love topping my bowls with avocado, hot sauce, or leftover pesto. You can also add extra grilled veggies or meat, or smoked salmon on top.

1 large spaghetti squash
   (see note)
Olive oil
1 teaspoon sea salt
1 teaspoon freshly ground black
   pepper
6 carrots, cut in half lengthwise
3 kale leaves, stemmed and torn
2 large organic, cage-free eggs
Optional topping: avacado, carrot
   tops, hot sauce, salsa, Tahini
   Sauce (000), or Homemade
   Summer Pesto (000)

Roast your spaghetti squash: Preheat the oven to 400°F and line a baking sheet with parchment paper. Cut the spaghetti squash in half lengthwise. Scoop out the seeds and discard. Rub all sides of the squash with olive oil and sprinkle the inside with the sea salt and pepper. Place, cut side down, on the prepared baking sheet and bake for 15 minutes. Remove the pan from the oven, add the carrots, and season with more olive oil, salt, and pepper. Return to the oven and bake for 20 to 25 minutes more, until you can easily poke the skin with a fork. Let cool for a few minutes before scraping the flesh off the sides, into noodles.

When ready to make your bowl, heat a splash of olive oil in a large skillet over medium-high heat. Place the carrots in the skillet to cook first. Add the spaghetti squash noodles next, just to warm. In the last minute, add the torn kale leaves and cook until they wilt, sprinkling everything with extra sea salt and pepper. Transfer to serving bowls.

Add a bit more oil to the pan and fry the eggs to your liking. Place on top of the spaghetti squash, adding whatever other toppings or sauces you'd like.

NOTE: The spaghetti squash and carrots can be roasted ahead of time and stored in the fridge until you are ready to assemble the bowls.

Seasonal Jam Dots

Makes 12 cookies

I have to restrain myself from making these too often, because I'll eat them all before anyone else gets to have one. They're amazing as a quick and healthy-ish breakfast with good amounts of fiber, protein, and healthy fat to keep you full through the morning, and without lots of sugar added, they're an upgraded sweet treat. I love using seedless raspberry and blackberry jam in this recipe, but feel free to use whatever you have on hand or whatever fruit preserve is in season at the time. I think these taste even better the next day . . . if you can handle waiting.

1 cup almond meal

½ cup gluten-free rolled oats

¼ cup coconut flour

6 tablespoons grass-fed butter, ghee, or coconut oil, melted

½ cup coconut sugar

1 tablespoon pure maple syrup

1 teaspoon baking powder

2 teaspoons pure vanilla extract

Juice-sweetened jam of your choice for filling

Preheat the oven to 350°F and line a baking sheet with parchment paper.

Combine all the ingredients, except the jam, in a medium bowl and mix together until combined. Squeeze a small handful of the batter together so it becomes moister. Form the dough into a ½-inch-thick round patty and gently push into the center to make a slight thumbprint. Repeat with the remaining dough. Bake for 10 to 15 minutes, until cookies are slightly brown on top.

Remove the cookies from the oven and add ¼ to ½ teaspoon jam to each thumbprint. Bake for another 3 to 5 minutes, until slightly browned and done to your liking. Remove from the pan and let cool for a few minutes on a wire rack before enjoying.

Cranberry Walnut Grain-Free Granola

Makes 8 to 10 servings

There is literally nothing better than homemade granola. It has so many uses and adds such a fun crunch to so many things: as a snack on its own, with milk of your choice, paired with whole-milk yogurt or coconut yogurt and fruit, or even sprinkled over salads in place of croutons. After the Pumpkin Chocolate Granola in the *Simply Real Health Cookbook* made headlines, I knew it was time to create another grain-free version that everyone could enjoy. Store this granola in an airtight container in the fridge for up to two weeks.

2 cups walnuts, roughly chopped

½ cup dried cranberries
    or cherries

¼ cup pumpkin seeds

3 tablespoons sunflower seeds

3 tablespoons hemp seeds or
    flaxseeds

3 tablespoons olive or coconut oil,
    melted

2 tablespoons pure maple syrup

1 tablespoon pure vanilla extract

1 tablespoon ground cinnamon

2 teaspoons pumpkin pie spice

1 teaspoon sea salt

Preheat the oven to 300°F and line a baking sheet with parchment paper.

Combine all the ingredients in a medium bowl and stir well until all the pieces are well coated.

Spread out the mixture on the prepared baking sheet and bake for 15 to 17 minutes, until golden brown, stirring as needed.

Savory Yogurt Bowls

Makes 2 servings

Hang tight with me for a moment and let me explain. A savory yogurt bowl? Why, yes. Because if you're truly hungry in the morning and not just eating out of habit, real food will sound good. So, before you knock it, give this one a try. It's perfect any time of day, but does a wonderful job in the morning of keeping your blood sugar stable and body fully nourished for whatever is ahead. The eggplant and the Garbanzo Bean Crunchies (page 158) can be cooked ahead of time for easy morning assembly.

Olive oil

1 small eggplant

Sea salt

Freshly ground black pepper

2 cups organic whole-milk Greek
　　or coconut yogurt

¼ cup Garbanzo Bean Crunchies
　　(page 158)

1 tablespoon finely chopped
　　chives (from about 2 stalks)

1 tablespoon finely chopped dill
　　(from about 2 sprigs)

½ lemon

Preheat a drizzle of olive oil in a large skillet over high heat.

Slice the eggplant into thin slices and place in a bowl. Drizzle with olive oil, sea salt, and pepper and rub to coat all surfaces. Add the eggplant slices to the hot skillet and cook for 10 to 12 minutes per side before flipping.

Meanwhile, split the yogurt between two serving bowls. When the eggplant is done, layer it into the bowl. Sprinkle with the Garbanzo Bean Crunchies, and add the chives, dill, sea salt and pepper to taste, and a squeeze of lemon juice to serve.

Grain-Free Seedy Bread

Makes 1 loaf

This hearty gluten- and grain-free bread is an amazing base for avocado toast with tomatoes and cucumber on top; for smoked salmon with goat cheese or hummus; for almond butter, banana, and cinnamon; or with mashed white beans pureed with garlic, lemon juice, red pepper flakes, and sea salt.

Feel free to use whatever seed combination you like here (a.k.a. whatever you have in your pantry). Pumpkin seeds, hemp seeds, poppy seeds, and so on, all work well. Or try adding some dried fruit and coconut flakes for a sweeter type of bread. If you do this, omit the cheese and nutritional yeast and add 2 tablespoons of pure maple syrup or honey instead. Add ½ cup gluten-free flour for a more traditional texture. Store the bread, covered, in the fridge for up to four days.

½ cup chia seeds

½ cup flaxseeds

½ cup sesame seeds

½ cup sunflower seeds

2 teaspoons Italian seasoning, or 2 tablespoons chopped fresh rosemary, basil, and thyme

1 tablespoon nutritional yeast or Parmesan

Sea salt

Freshly ground black pepper

Preheat the oven to 400°F. Line a 9-by-5-inch loaf pan with parchment paper.

Combine all the seeds in a medium bowl, add the Italian seasoning, nutritional yeast, salt and pepper to taste, and 1 cup of water, and mix well. Let the mixture sit for a minute or two, until it is slightly sticky. Wet your fingers and evenly press the mixture into the prepared loaf pan. Bake for 40 minutes, or until the crust is slightly browned on top. Let cool in the pan before slicing and toasting to use however you want.

Sweet Potato Morning Muffins

Makes 12 muffins

This is one of my all-time favorite recipes. The sweet potatoes or yams can be roasted ahead of time to speed up the process (you might as well make a couple for the week while you're at it). You can freeze extras for quick morning breakfast treats!

1 large or 2 smaller sweet potatoes
   or yams (see note)
½ cup olive oil
½ cup Homemade Nut Milk
   (page 42) or milk of your
   choice
1 teaspoon pure vanilla extract
¾ cup pure maple syrup,
   plus more for brushing
   (optional)
1 cup gluten-free flour blend
1 cup almond meal
1½ tablespoons ground
   cinnamon
2 teaspoons baking powder
2 teaspoons baking soda
½ teaspoon sea salt
Coconut oil spray (optional)

Preheat the oven to 400°F and line a baking sheet with parchment paper. Place the sweet potatoes on the prepared baking sheet and roast for 35 to 40 minutes, until you can easily prick them with a fork.

Scoop out the potato flesh, discard the skin, then place the flesh in a bowl along with the olive oil, milk, vanilla, and maple syrup. Whisk with an electric mixer until smooth. In a separate bowl, stir together the flour, almond meal, cinnamon, baking powder, baking soda, and sea salt. Add the dry ingredients to the wet, mixing well to combine.

Line 12 wells of a muffin tin or spray with coconut oil. Scoop the batter into the prepared tins and bake for 25 to 30 minutes, until a toothpick inserted into the center of a muffin comes out clean. During the last 5 minutes of baking, brush the muffin tops with extra maple syrup, if desired.

NOTE: Short on time? Try it with a can of pureed butternut squash instead.

BETTER THAN BRUNCH
GFTs (Gluten-Free Treats) and Weekend Winners

Mini Pumpkin Spice Doughnuts (or Muffins)   75

Spicy Tomato Shakshuka   76

Skillet Potato Pancake with Green Onions and Chives   79

Sweet Potato Waffles with Fried Eggs   80

Apple Pie Bars   83

Butternut Squash and Cardamom Pancakes   84

Blackberry Scones   86

Zucchini Bread   87

Life-Changing Gluten-Free Waffles   89

Huevos Rancheros Bake   90

Homemade Corn Muffins   93

Kale Feta Bread   94

The best start to your weekend, no reservations required.

Mini Pumpkin Spice Doughnuts (or Muffins)

Makes 24 mini doughnuts or mini muffins, 12 muffins, or 1 loaf

This recipe can also be made as a pumpkin loaf, baked for 45 minutes to 1 hour in a loaf pan, or regular-size muffins, baked for 23 to 25 minutes. But mini doughnuts are just so fun, so if you have a mini doughnut pan on hand, that's what I would suggest. If you are using icing, make the doughnuts, muffins, or loaf first, then make the icing while you let them cool. If not using icing, I recommend serving the doughnuts, muffins, or loaf warm with a big pat of butter on top.

Coconut oil spray or grass-fed butter

1 cup pure pumpkin puree

2 large organic, cage-free eggs, beaten

¾ cup coconut oil, melted

1 teaspoon pure vanilla extract

1 cup gluten-free flour blend

⅔ cup almond meal

1 cup granulated or coconut sugar

1 tablespoon ground cinnamon

2 teaspoons pumpkin pie spice

1 teaspoon baking soda

ICING (OPTIONAL)

3 tablespoons powdered sugar

2 tablespoons coconut oil

Preheat the oven to 350°F. Spray a 24-well mini doughnut pan, 12-well muffin tin, or 9-by-5-inch loaf pan with coconut oil spray or butter the pan.

Stir together the pumpkin puree, eggs, oil, and vanilla in a medium bowl. Stir together the flour, almond meal, granulated sugar, cinnamon, pumpkin pie spice, and baking soda in a separate medium bowl. Add the dry mixture to the wet and stir to combine. Pour into the prepared pan. If making mini doughnuts, bake for about 25 minutes, or until the center is cooked through. Let cool for a few minutes on a wire rack while you make the icing, if using.

Prepare the icing: Combine the sugar and coconut oil in a saucepan over low heat and whisk together as they melt for 7 minutes. Remove from the heat and let thicken for 1 to 2 minutes before drizzling on top of your doughnuts, muffins, or loaf.

Spicy Tomato Shakshuka

Makes 2 or 3 servings

Shakshuka is a savory tomato egg bake, meant for dipping and sharing. For extra protein, add cooked sausage or shredded chicken. Feta, hot sauce, or chopped cilantro would all be great topping additions. You can also serve this dish for dinner over rice or with toasted gluten-free bread.

Olive oil

1 onion, chopped

1 bell pepper, seeded and chopped

3 garlic cloves, chopped

4 kale leaves, stemmed and torn

1 teaspoon ground cumin

1 teaspoon smoked paprika

1 teaspoon sea salt

½ teaspoon freshly ground black pepper

1 (28-ounce) can whole or crushed tomatoes, drained of excess liquid

2 to 3 large organic, cage-free eggs

Preheat the oven to 375°F.

Heat a bit of olive oil in an ovenproof skillet over medium heat. Add the onion and bell pepper and cook for 5 to 7 minutes, until soft. Add the garlic, kale, cumin, paprika, salt, and black pepper and cook for another minute. Add the tomatoes and stir well to combine, breaking them up with a wooden spoon. Simmer for 5 minutes, then use the back of a spoon to make two or three holes in the mixture. Crack an egg into each hole. Transfer the dish to the oven and bake for 7 to 12 minutes, until the eggs have set to your liking. Serve in the skillet.

Skillet Potato Pancake with Green Onions and Chives

Makes 6 to 8 servings

This is a excellent make-ahead dish for breakfast, brunch, or dinner. Just follow the instructions below, pop the finished pancake in the refrigerator, and heat it up in a skillet when you're ready to eat. You can also use this batter to make smaller single serving–size pancakes. Great toppings and sides include Greek yogurt, homemade tzatziki sauce, fried eggs, grilled chicken, sausage, a green salad, or roasted vegetables. Also try this recipe using yams, sweet potatoes, or other root veggies in place of the potatoes, for a fun twist.

4 medium russet potatoes

3 green onions, chopped

8 fresh chive stalks, chopped

1 cup fresh parsley leaves, chopped

4 large organic, cage-free eggs

2 teaspoons sea salt

1 teaspoon freshly ground black pepper

¼ cup gluten-free flour blend (optional)

Olive oil

Shred the potatoes with a food processor or a box grater. Drain and squeeze out any extra liquid. Place the potatoes as well as all the remaining ingredients, except the flour and olive oil, in a medium bowl and stir well to combine. Drain any excess water again. If the mixture is still wet, add up to ¼ cup of the flour and mix well until all the liquid is absorbed.

Heat a generous splash of olive oil in a large skillet over medium-high heat. Add the potato mixture, spread evenly in the pan, and press down with the back of a spoon. Cook until the bottom starts to brown, about 10 minutes. Place a plate over the skillet and flip the potato pancake, sliding it back into the pan to cook the second side. Cook for another 5 to 10 minutes, until crispy and warmed through.

Sweet Potato Waffles with Fried Eggs

Makes 3 to 4 servings (2 waffles per person)

Think: sweet potato fries, in a waffle form: what's not to love here? I love this savory-style brunch dish topped with fried eggs, hot sauce, and arugula, or on its own, but feel free to add any other toppings you'd like, such as turkey bacon, sliced tomatoes, natural ketchup, or pesto. Don't have a waffle iron? Turn this batter into savory pancakes.

WAFFLES

6 cups cooked sweet potato, from about 6 medium sweet potatoes (see note)

6 tablespoons coconut flour or gluten-free flour blend

4 large organic, cage-free eggs, beaten

Coconut oil spray

2 cups arugula (optional)

3 green onions, finely chopped (optional)

1 teaspoon sea salt

1 teaspoon freshly ground black pepper

FRIED EGGS

Coconut or olive oil

4 to 6 large organic, cage-free eggs

Prepare the waffles: Combine the sweet potato, flour, and 4 eggs in a large bowl and mix well.

Preheat a waffle iron and spray with coconut oil spray. Pour the batter into the heated iron, distributing it evenly. Depending on your waffle iron, you may find it helpful to flip the waffles halfway through. Transfer the waffles to a serving platter and keep warm while you fry the eggs.

Prepare the fried eggs: Heat the coconut oil in a large skillet. When hot, crack the eggs into the skillet and cook until done to your liking. Plate the cooked eggs on top of the waffles, topping with the arugula and green onions, if using, and sea salt and pepper.

NOTE: The sweet potatoes can be cooked ahead of time. I roast mine whole on a parchment-lined baking sheet in a 400°F oven for 35 to 40 minutes, or until you can easily poke them with a fork. Remove from the oven and let cool to make it easier to scoop out the flesh.

Apple Pie Bars

Makes 9 square bars

Like apple pie, but upgraded. These bars are an amazing weekend treat with a dollop of Greek yogurt on the side, or with a scoop of vanilla gelato or coconut ice cream for dessert.

Coconut or olive oil for the pan

4 medium apples, peeled, seeded and cubed

2 teaspoons ground cinnamon

Juice of 1 small lemon

1 cup plus 2 tablespoons gluten-free flour blend

1 teaspoon baking powder

Pinch of sea salt

Pinch of freshly grated nutmeg

10 tablespoons grass-fed butter, melted

1 cup coconut sugar, muscovado sugar, or unrefined cane sugar

2 large organic, cage-free eggs

1 teaspoon pure vanilla extract

Preheat the oven to 325°F and grease an 8-inch square baking dish or line it with parchment paper.

Place the cubed apples in a large bowl, toss with 1 teaspoon of the cinnamon and the lemon juice, and set aside.

Combine the flour, baking powder, sea salt, remaining teaspoon of cinnamon, and the nutmeg in a medium bowl and mix well, then set aside. Combine the butter, sugar, eggs, and vanilla in a separate large bowl, mixing or beating well after each addition. Add the dry ingredients to the wet and mix well to combine.

Scrape about two-thirds of the batter into the bowl of apples and mix to coat all the apples with the batter. It will be very chunky. Scrape the remaining one-third of the cake batter into the prepared baking dish and spread into an even layer, using a spatula. Scrape the apple-packed cake batter on top of the first layer and spread out evenly.

Cover the pan tightly with foil and place in the center of the oven. Bake for 20 minutes. Remove the foil and bake for another 20 to 25 minutes, until the center is set and an inserted toothpick comes out clean.

Remove from the oven and allow the bars to cool in the pan for at least 10 to 15 minutes before slicing.

Butternut Squash and Cardamom Pancakes

Makes 2 to 3 servings (about 8 pancakes)

These (almost) too simple and healthy pancakes are so good served with natural peanut or almond butter, homemade whipped cream, seasonal fruit, or a drizzle of pure maple syrup or raw honey. You can also replace the squash with pumpkin and remove the cardamom for pickier palates.

1 large ripe banana

¼ cup butternut squash puree

2 large organic, cage-free eggs

¼ teaspoon baking powder

¼ teaspoon ground cinnamon

¼ teaspoon ground cardamom

1 tablespoon grass-fed butter or coconut oil

Combine all the ingredients, except the butter, in a blender and blend until smooth. Alternatively, mash together the banana and squash by hand in a medium bowl, then add the eggs, baking powder, and spices and mix well. Transfer the mixture to a measuring cup with a spout, for easy pouring.

Heat 1 tablespoon of butter on a griddle or in a cast-iron skillet over medium-high heat. Once hot, pour the batter as you would for normal mini pancakes, about four at a time, and cook, flipping halfway when slightly browned, about 4 minutes on each side.

Blackberry Scones

Makes 12 scones

If I could eat one baked-good for the rest of my life, scones would be it. I adore them served warm or toasted with an extra smear of butter or ghee on top. Feel free to swap in blueberries, strawberries, rhubarb, or whatever other seasonal fruit you like. (See photograph on page 5.)

1 to 2 cups blackberries

1 cup almond meal

1 cup gluten-free rolled oats

1 cup small coconut flakes

8 tablespoons grass-fed butter, melted

¼ cup pure maple syrup or coconut sugar

1 tablespoon pure vanilla extract

Preheat the oven to 350°F and line a baking sheet with parchment paper.

Mix all the ingredients together in a medium bowl and form with your hands into triangular scones, squeezing the batter together, if needed. Bake for 25 minutes, or until golden brown on top.

Zucchini Bread

Makes 1 loaf

The queen of sneaky veggies that get zero complaints, this loaf is amazing, and is one of my go-tos anytime I want to make a treat I feel great about sitting on my counter. You can also add a handful of chopped walnuts, or chocolate chips. Or make into muffins, baking for 20 to 25 minutes.

Coconut oil spray

2 medium zucchini

2 ripe bananas

½ cup coconut oil, melted

1⅔ cups gluten-free flour blend

1 cup coconut sugar or organic cane sugar

2 large organic, cage-free eggs

1 teaspoon baking soda

1 teaspoon ground cinnamon

Sprinkle of sea salt

Preheat the oven to 375°F. Spray a 9-by-5-inch loaf pan with coconut oil spray.

Grate the zucchini through a large box grater, using the larger holes. Place the zucchini shreds and bananas in a blender and blend gently until combined, without overprocessing. Transfer to a large bowl and add the remaining ingredients. Mix well. Pour the batter into the prepared loaf pan and bake for 1 hour, or until an inserted toothpick comes out clean.

Life-Changing Gluten-Free Waffles

Makes 4 servings (2 waffles per person)

This batter can be made ahead of time (up to a day before you need it) and stored in the fridge. For the best results, place the batter in the fridge for at least 10 minutes before you cook it, so it can thicken. Optional toppings include homemade whipped cream (or the coconut whipped cream from the *Simply Real Health Cookbook*), berries, bananas, coconut flakes, natural peanut or almond butter, honey, pure maple syrup, or what we call "husband style" around here—with a big sprinkle of dark chocolate chips mixed right into the batter itself.

1 ¾ cups gluten-free flour blend

1 ¾ cups almond milk or organic whole milk

2 large organic, cage-free eggs, whisked first in a bowl

8 tablespoons grass-fed butter, ghee, or coconut oil, melted

1 tablespoon baking powder

1 teaspoon pure vanilla extract

Tiny pinch of sea salt

Coconut oil spray

Combine all the ingredients, except the coconut oil spray, in a large bowl and mix well. Refrigerate the batter for 10 minutes.

Preheat a waffle iron and spray with coconut oil spray. Spread the batter evenly on the heated iron, close, and cook until the waffles start to crisp. When the bottom part is crisped, flip the waffles and crisp the top for 2 to 3 minutes, depending on your waffle maker. Serve hot with toppings of your choice.

Huevos Rancheros Bake

Makes 6 to 8 servings

Hands down, this is the perfect one-pan meal for hosting. Assemble the dish, minus the eggs, ahead of time and store in the fridge. When ready to cook, add the eggs as directed and bake. I love serving it with sliced avocado on top and hot sauce on the side. Pair with a green salad and you're all ready to go.

One 16-ounce jar natural enchilada sauce (you will have some leftover)

12 organic white or blue corn tortillas

One 15-ounce can refried pinto beans

2 cups shredded organic cheddar cheese

1 bunch fresh cilantro, chopped, plus more for serving

1 jalapeño pepper, sliced (optional)

6 to 8 large organic, cage-free eggs

Sea salt

Freshly ground black pepper

1 avocado, sliced, for serving

Preheat the oven to 400°F.

Spread a thin layer of the enchilada sauce in a 9-by-13-inch casserole dish. Layer six tortillas into the dish, trying not to overlap them too much (you can break them into pieces to fit). Spread with a thin layer of enchilada sauce, refried beans, cheese, and cilantro, and repeat with another layer until the tortillas are used and the top is sprinkled with cheese. Add the jalapeño slices on top, if desired.

When ready to bake, make six to eight little holes with the back of a spoon for the eggs to nestle into. Crack an egg into each hole.

Bake for 45 to 50 minutes, until the eggs are done to your liking. Sprinkle with salt and black pepper, top with avacodo, and garnish with extra chopped cilantro to serve.

Homemade Corn Muffins

Makes 12 muffins

This tasty little recipe is inspired by one of my favorite restaurants in Cabo, Mexico, that serves these instead of bread. They are amazing slathered with grass-fed butter or ghee when warm.

1¼ cups organic cornmeal

1 cup gluten-free flour blend

1 large organic, cage-free egg

1 cup almond or coconut milk

½ cup coconut sugar

1 tablespoon baking powder

½ teaspoon sea salt, plus more for sprinkling

4 tablespoons grass-fed butter or ghee, melted, or olive oil

Preheat the oven to 350°F and grease 12 wells of a muffin tin or use paper liners.

Mix together all the ingredients in a medium bowl with ½ cup of water. Pour the batter into the prepared muffin tin and bake for 28 minutes, until the tops of the muffins are slightly brown and an inserted toothpick comes out clean. Remove from the oven and sprinkle with sea salt when done.

Kale Feta Bread

Makes 6 to 8 servings

Eat this bread warm and toasted, with big slabs of grass-fed butter or ghee melted on top; open-faced sandwich style, topped with avocado, tomatoes, and a fried egg; or as an easy dinner side. Morning, noon, or night, this bread can work in so many ways, and is an easy way to get some extra leafy greens in your life. I love using dill, but feel free to use whatever herbs you like. Store, covered, in the fridge for up seven days, slicing and toasting as you need to.

Coconut or olive oil spray or
butter, for pan

2 large organic, cage-free eggs,
beaten

1 cup whole-milk Greek yogurt
or coconut milk yogurt

½ cup olive oil

¾ cup gluten-free flour

¾ cup almond meal

1½ tablespoons baking powder

1 to 2 teaspoons sea salt

1 to 2 teaspoons freshly ground
black pepper

2 to 3 dinosaur kale leaves,
stemmed and finely chopped

½ cup feta, crumbled

¼ cup walnuts, chopped

½ cup chopped fresh herbs,
such as basil, tarragon or dill
(optional)

Preheat the oven to 350°F and oil a 9-by-5-inch loaf pan with coconut or olive oil spray, or butter it.

Combine the eggs, yogurt, and oil in a medium bowl, and the flour, almond meal, baking powder, sea salt, and pepper in a large bowl. Mix well, separately, then pour the wet ingredients into the dry, and stir well to combine. Stir in the kale, feta, walnuts, and herbs.

Pour the batter into the pan, flatten evenly with the back of a spoon, and bake for 50 to 55 minutes, or until golden brown on top. Remove from the oven and let cool before slicing.

Thai Crab Cucumber Salad, page 128

NOURISHING NOONS

LUNCHLADY RECIPES
Everyday Gold for Busy Weeks

The Real Greek Salad   100

Salmon Niçoise Salad with Sarah's Daily Basil Dressing   102

Summer Picnic Poblano Salad   105

Pesto, Quinoa, and Tomato Salad   106

The Everyday Chicken Salad   109

The Cobb Job Salad   110

Quinoa, Feta, Dill, and Garbanzo Bean Salad   112

The Lemon Feta Salad   115

Baja Chopped Caesar Salad   116

Seared Ahi and Crab Ceviche 119

Roasted Cauliflower, Carrot, and Tahini Salad   120

The Sister A.G.T.O. Salad   123

The Fall Salad You Won't Be Able to Quit   124

Kale and Quinoa Salad with Squash, Apricots, and Bacon   127

Thai Crab Cucumber Salad   128

Cozy Roasted Parsnip Soup   129

3-Ingredient Tomato Soup   131

Healthy Veggie Noodle Pho   132

Roasted Kabocha Squash Soup   135

I have just three simple rules when it comes to lunch:
1. I eat one daily.
2. Veggies must be involved.
3. No wimpy or boring salads allowed.

The Real Greek Salad

Makes 4 servings

Our honeymoon in the Greek Islands taught me two things: (1) a real Greek salad was nothing at all like the Greek salads at home, and (2) I had been severely missing out. After eating one every single day and leaving the trip wanting more, I made it my mission as soon as we got home to re-create this Mediterranean magic. I took notes the whole trip: how each *taverna* would have its own twist, though the base was always the same. Pure, simple, and almost impossible to eat without a side of salty olives, a cold glass of rosé, and some grilled fish, it's probably why this dish has earned a spot on our weekly summer rotation.

This salad keeps well in the fridge for a few days with just the vinegar on it. Hold off on the olive oil and feta until you're ready to eat. I adore this salad straight up, or spooned over a big bowl of arugula or mixed greens. Add-ins, such as gigante or white beans, grilled chicken, pepperoncini, olives, capers, or roasted potatoes, though not traditional, are all delicious as well.

1 green bell pepper, seeded and
    thinly sliced
1 pint cherry tomatoes, halved
2 English cucumbers, peeled,
    seeded, and sliced
Leaves from 4 to 6 oregano sprigs,
    finely chopped
1 teaspoon dried or chopped fresh
    parsley, basil, or mixed Italian
    herbs
1 tablespoon red wine vinegar
High quality olive oil
1 block (about 2 ounces) feta,
    sliced into 4 pieces
2 grilled chicken breasts or
    other protein of your choice
    (optional)
1 teaspoon sea salt
½ teaspoon freshly ground black
    pepper

Combine the bell pepper, tomatoes, cucumbers, oregano, and parsley in a large bowl and drizzle with the vinegar. Toss to mix together well. When ready to serve, add olive oil to taste and the feta, and chicken, if using, on top and sprinkle with the sea salt and pepper.

RITUAL #5: BECOME A #LUNCHLADY

THE RITUAL: Make lunch a nonnegotiable in your life, a grounding point in your day that you take the time for, even if you only have 10 minutes to spare. If it's not something you already do, plan ahead: bring something with you, or think through where you will be mid-day and what the healthy options might be near you. Not thinking about lunch until you're too hungry will usually end in a quick, mindless meal of mediocre food that makes you hungrier in the hours to follow.

For most of my life, lunch seemed like a waste of time. I ate a big breakfast like I was supposed to. And a midmorning snack, too. And then, I'd try and power through the afternoon, telling myself it was way more efficient to eat smaller meals or snacks, instead of a real meal. A.k.a. a protein bar here, a piece of fruit there, and maybe some cheese or nuts.

But you know where it would lead me? At 4 p.m. with crazy eyes, rummaging through the pantry for anything I could find. I'd eat a lot, usually ruining my dinner appetite, which would make me starving and ready for a big meal in the morning, continuing the cycle endlessly.

I didn't know that an easy solution could come from one quick and simple upgrade: eating an actual, real lunch. And not allowing myself to glorify the phrase "I'm too busy." Because I *do* actually have time for the things that matter most, and my energy, decidedly, is one of them.

It's something I had to learn the hard way: that eating an actual lunch with real substance versus snacking throughout the day can change your life.

Truth: Busy days mean it's even *more* important for me to be a good #lunchlady, not less.

Becoming a real #lunchlady, meaning eating a real lunch every day, will help keep your blood sugar calm and your energy steady. Side benefits? No need to snack, less time spent thinking about food in your day, fewer 4 p.m. hangry episodes, daily sugar cravings, and those unnecessary afternoon coffees.

Salmon Niçoise Salad with Sarah's Daily Basil Dressing

Makes 2 servings

This salad is such a great example of a big and beautiful meal, instead of a side of boring lettuce. The key to amazing salads like this? A variety of textures: some parts crunchy (the green beans), some parts creamy (the potatoes and avocado and dressing), some parts salty (olives), and some parts nice and light (the tomatoes and lettuce). Also key are ingredients of substance and nutrient density (the eggs, avocado, potatoes, and any protein you may add), to help keep you full for hours afterward. All components of this salad can be prepped ahead of time—just hold off on the avocado and adding the dressing until you're ready to eat. I like to double this recipe and divide it among a few glass containers for easy grab-and-go lunches throughout the week.

2 cups baby potatoes, halved

2 large organic, cage-free eggs

Sea salt

8 ounces green beans, trimmed

4 to 6 cups butter lettuce or mixed
    greens

3 Roma tomatoes, seeded and
    chopped

8 ounces wild salmon fillet,
    grilled, baked, or roasted

8 to 10 olives, pitted

1 avocado, sliced

½ cup Daily Basil Dressing
    (recipe follows)

Bring 6 cups of water to a boil in a medium stockpot, then add the potatoes and eggs and a generous sprinkle of sea salt. Lower the heat to medium and let cook for 10 to 12 minutes, until you can almost poke the potatoes easily with a fork. Remove the eggs and set aside. Add the green beans to the pot, and cook along with the potatoes for another 3 to 4 minutes. Drain the veggies in a colander in the sink and let cool. Peel the eggs and slice in half.

Layer a bowl or resealable containers with all the salad ingredients, except the avocado and dressing. Add the avocado and dressing when ready to serve.

Daily Basil Dressing

Makes about 1 cup dressing

I love to keep this dressing in the fridge and build on it as the week goes by, so I always make twice as much as I need, as written below. Want a thicker pesto dressing? Just add a few handfuls of nuts and/or grated cheese and blend. This is also amazing with any other extra herbs, or made with garlic-infused olive oil.

Add **4 cups fresh basil, ¾ cup extra virgin olive oil, 2 tablespoons Dijon mustard, ¼ cup red wine vinegar (or juice of ½ lemon), 1 teaspoon sea salt, and 1 teaspoon freshly ground black pepper** to a blender and blend until well mixed.

Summer Picnic Poblano Salad

Serves 8

This is the perfect make-ahead, picnic-style salad. This baby pairs great with chicken, sausage, grilled shrimp or steak, or with the addition of black or pinto beans, too. It's also amazing as a taco filling.

2 poblano or green bell peppers, seeded and chopped

2 red bell peppers, seeded and chopped

Kernels from 4 ears organic corn

Juice of 2 limes

Garlic-infused or regular olive oil

2 grilled chicken breasts or other protein of your choice (optional)

2 avocados, cubed

Leaves from 5 oregano sprigs, chopped

½ cup chopped fresh cilantro

Sea salt

Freshly ground black pepper

Combine the poblano and bell peppers and corn kernels in a large serving bowl. Drizzle with the lime juice and about 1 tablespoon of the garlic-infused olive oil and toss well to combine. At this point, you can also divide the salad among airtight containers and store in the fridge for easy lunches.

Before serving, top with the chicken, if using, garnish with the avocado, oregano, and cilantro, and season to taste with sea salt and black pepper.

Pesto, Quinoa, and Tomato Salad

Makes 6 servings

This is a perfect make-ahead dish for quick and easy lunches or dinners, and makes a great base for such add-ins as grilled chicken, clean sausage, or arugula.

1½ cups uncooked quinoa

Sea salt

1½ cups Homemade Summer Pesto (recipe follows)

2 cups cherry tomatoes, halved

Sprinkle of pine nuts

Freshly ground black pepper

2 grilled chicken breasts or other protein of your choice (optional)

½ cup chopped fresh basil (optional)

Combine the quinoa and 3 cups of water in a small saucepan. Add a pinch of sea salt, cover, and bring to a boil. Turn off the heat and let the quinoa cook, covered, for about 10 minutes, or until all the water is absorbed.

When the quinoa is done, fluff with a fork and transfer to a serving bowl. Stir in the pesto, tomatoes, and pine nuts and sprinkle with a generous amount of sea salt and pepper. Top with the chicken, if using, and garnish with the chopped basil, if using, to serve.

Homemade Summer Pesto

Makes about 1 cup pesto

This is the perfect easy dressing for any salad or to use as a marinade, pizza topping, or dip. Store in the fridge in a sealed container for up to two weeks. I highly suggest doubling this recipe and freezing any extra in silicone ice cube trays for later use.

Blend **4 ounces fresh basil, ½ cup shredded Parmesan, ¼ cup pine nuts or nuts of your choice, ¼ cup olive oil**, and the **juice of 1 lemon** in a blender, generously adding **sea salt** and **pepper** to taste.

The Everyday Chicken Salad

Makes 4 servings

This salad is perfect over mixed greens, spinach, or arugula or served in lettuce cups for a quick easy lunch. It keeps well for five to seven days in the fridge. I adore using Homemade Avocado Mayo (recipe follows), or Primal Kitchen's avocado mayo if you're short on time, in this recipe.

1 large or 2 medium organic
    chicken breasts
Sea salt
Freshly ground black pepper
1 cup red grapes, halved,
    or ½ medium green apple,
    seeded and chopped
1 cup walnuts or pecans, chopped
Juice of ¼ lemon
¼ cup chopped fresh tarragon
3 celery ribs, chopped
½ cup Homemade Avocado Mayo
    (recipe follows) or a clean
    store-bought brand

Preheat the oven to 350°F. Place the chicken in a baking dish, season with salt and pepper, and bake until cooked through, 20 to 25 minutes, depending on thickness. Remove the chicken from the oven and let cool before slicing or shredding.

In the meantime, mix together all the remaining ingredients in a bowl, adding a generous amount of sea salt and pepper to taste. Add the chicken and mix until well combined. Store in the fridge until ready to eat.

Homemade Avocado Mayo

Makes ¾ cup

This is such a great versatile recipe to have around, without the low-grade canola or soybean oil that's found in most store-bought mayonnaise. This spread is perfect for sandwiches, to mix into tuna or chicken salad, or to use in place of regular mayo in any recipe that calls for it. Keeps well in the fridge for up to one week.

Add **1 avocado (peeled and pitted), juice of ½ lemon, 2 teaspoons Dijon mustard,** and **½ teaspoon sea salt** to a blender or food processor and process, then slowly add **⅓ cup olive oil** as the machine runs until the mixture thickens. Add more lemon juice, if desired. Store in a sealed container in the fridge.

The Cobb Job Salad

Makes 4 to 6 servings

These salad components can be made ahead of time for easy assembly of hearty lunches or a quick dinner. Just hold off on adding the avocado and dressing until you're ready to eat.

3 large organic, cage-free eggs

1 organic chicken breast

Sea salt

Freshly ground black pepper

6 strips nitrate-free turkey bacon

2 heads Bibb, butter, or romaine
    lettuce

1 avocado, sliced

1 heirloom tomato, sliced,
    or ½ cup halved cherry
    tomatoes

½ cup sprouts or pea shoots

¼ cup blue cheese, crumbled

DRESSING

½ cup olive oil

2 tablespoons red wine vinegar

2 tablespoons Dijon mustard

Sea salt

Freshly ground black pepper

Bring 4 cups of water to a boil in each of two saucepans. Place the eggs in one of the pots to hard boil for 9 minutes, then remove from the pot and let cool before peeling and slicing in half. Meanwhile, place the chicken breast in the other pot of boiling water and cook for 9 to 12 minutes, until cooked through. Remove the chicken and shred the meat with a fork. Season to taste with sea salt and pepper and set aside.

Cook the bacon, then transfer to paper towels to drain. Then crumble it.

Prepare the dressing: Whisk together all the dressing ingredients in a small bowl or mug.

Wash, tear, and dry the lettuce and place it in a large salad bowl. Add the eggs, chicken, bacon, avocado, tomato, sprouts, and blue cheese to the lettuce and toss with the dressing to serve.

Quinoa, Feta, Dill, and Garbanzo Bean Salad

Makes 6 to 8 servings

I love this salad so much—it keeps well for multiple days in the fridge and has so much flavor. It is a great way to turn pantry staples into a meal, and to use up any extra herbs you have on hand. It's also the perfect base for whatever you have in your fridge already. Fun additions to this recipe could include chopped tomatoes, chopped apricots, olives, or shredded chicken.

2 cups uncooked quinoa

Sea salt

¼ cup chopped chives

¼ cup chopped fresh dill

¼ cup chopped fresh mint

One 15-ounce can garbanzo
   beans, rinsed and drained,
   or 2 cups cooked

6 tablespoons olive oil

¼ cup red wine vinegar

Freshly ground black pepper

6 to 8 cups (or one 5-ounce
   package) arugula or spinach

½ cup feta, crumbled

Combine the quinoa and 4 cups of water in a small saucepan. Add a pinch of sea salt, cover, and bring to a boil. Turn off the heat and let the quinoa cook, covered, for about 10 minutes, or until all the water is absorbed.

In the meantime, place the herbs and garbanzo beans in a bowl. Drizzle with the olive oil and vinegar, and sprinkle generously with sea salt and pepper. When the quinoa is done cooking, let it cool for a few minutes before fluffing and adding it to the bowl. When you are ready to serve, gently fold in the arugula and sprinkle the feta on top.

OTHER VARIATIONS FOR QUICK AND EASY BOWLS

I love to batch roast veggies, grill or bake some protein, cook a grain, and make a sauce on Sundays. I store all the ingredients separately in the fridge for easy bowl making throughout the week.

- Roasted Brussels sprouts + beets + winter squash + quinoa + arugula + hummus
- Roasted potatoes + sautéed mushrooms + grilled chicken + rice + spinach + pesto
- Roasted cauliflower + carrot + sweet potato + pickled veggies or sauerkraut + spinach + buckwheat + tahini sauce
- Roasted winter squash + sautéed green beans + kale + millet + peanut sauce

The Lemon Feta Salad

Makes 4 servings

This salad is the epitome of spring, and more evidence that salads can in fact be the main meal, if loaded with a variety of different textures—creaminess from the avocado and feta, crunchiness from the snap peas, and a bit of peppery spice with the radishes. This one is always a hit, no matter the occasion!

I love making twice as much dressing as needed for this salad because it's so good on so many other things for the week: a dip or sauce for potatoes, rice, quinoa, chicken, lamb, steak, shrimp, roasted or raw veggies, and so on.

LEMON FETA DRESSING

¼ cup olive oil

¼ cup crumbled feta

Juice of ½ lemon

2 tablespoons chopped dill

4 chive stalks, chopped

½ teaspoon sea salt

¼ teaspoon freshly ground black
    pepper

SALAD

1 head butter or red leaf lettuce,
    torn

1 ripe avocado, peeled, pitted, and
    cubed or sliced

½ cup snap peas, ends removed
    and halved

2 or 3 radishes, thinly sliced

4 chive stalks, finely chopped

¼ cup crumbled feta

Prepare the dressing: Place all the dressing ingredients in a blender and blend. Store in a glass jar in the fridge for up to a week.

Prepare the salad: Combine all the salad ingredients in a serving bowl, pour the dressing on top, and toss gently to serve.

Baja Chopped Caesar Salad

Makes 4 to 6 servings

This salad is awesome paired with grilled wild salmon, shrimp, or chicken. Serve as described for a fun presentation, or chop the lettuce and toss like a traditional salad. The dressing and protein can be cooked ahead of time, and the lettuce washed and patted when you're ready to serve.

BAJA CAESAR DRESSING

½ cup whole-milk Greek yogurt, or unsweetened coconut milk yogurt

¼ cup olive oil

Juice of 2 limes

2 teaspoons gluten-free Worcestershire sauce

2 teaspoons anchovy paste

2 teaspoons Dijon mustard

1 teaspoon sea salt

1 teaspoon freshly ground black pepper

SALAD

1 large or 2 small heads romaine lettuce, halved lengthwise

2 or 3 radishes, thinly sliced

1 ripe avocado, peeled, pitted, and cubed or sliced

¼ cup chopped fresh cilantro

10 to 12 ounces grilled wild salmon or other protein of your choice (optional)

Feta or grated Parmesan for serving (optional)

Prepare the dressing: Whisk together all the dressing ingredients in a small bowl.

Arrange the salad: Assemble the romaine halves on a large platter and drizzle with the dressing. Arrange the radishes, avocado, and cilantro on top. If using, top with protein of your choice and sprinkle with feta or Parmesan to serve.

Seared Ahi and Crab Ceviche

Makes 4 to 6 servings

This little combination is one of my all-time favorite creations I've cooked up over the last few years. I love making it for the week for quick and easy lunches or dinners; it's perfect wrapped in lettuce, over salad greens, or as a taco filling, too. For parties, it's fun to serve in small glasses for an impressive app that looks as if you spent hours making it. This ceviche is best if made one to two hours before serving, and it keeps well for two to three days in the fridge. You can use other seafood of your choice, and include add-ins such as hot sauce, avocado, sesame seeds, and so on.

1 English cucumber, peeled, seeded, and cubed

1 small jicama, peeled and cut into $\frac{1}{2}$-inch cubes

8 Roma tomatoes, seeded and cut into $\frac{1}{2}$-inch cubes

4 ounces crab or small shrimp, cooked

2 green onions, finely chopped

1 cup cilantro leaves, chopped

Juice of 2 limes

2 teaspoons sea salt, plus a pinch for ahi

1 teaspoon freshly ground black pepper, plus a pinch for ahi

Olive oil, for skillet

Three 8-ounce wild ahi tuna steaks

Place the cucumber, jicama, and tomatoes in a large bowl. Add the crab, green onions, cilantro, lime juice, sea salt, and pepper and stir gently to combine.

Heat a bit of olive oil in a large skillet over high heat. When hot, sprinkle the ahi with a pinch of sea salt and pepper and place in the skillet to sear for about 2 minutes, or until cooked to your liking. Flip the fish and sear on the second side for 1 to 2 minutes, then remove from the skillet and let cool on a plate.

Slice the ahi into small cubes and add to the rest of the ingredients. Keep cold until ready to serve.

Roasted Cauliflower, Carrot, and Tahini Salad

Makes 4 servings

This is one of my favorite fall and winter make-ahead salads. It keeps well in the fridge for up to seven days, and is so good on its own, as a side dish, or on top of salad greens. Optional additions include shredded chicken, cooked sausage, or white beans, for a heartier meal. Use the extra tahini dressing in any other recipe you'd like! It makes a perfect marinade for fish, chicken, or other veggies, or a great salad dressing.

SALAD

2 heads cauliflower, cut into
    florets
10 to 12 carrots, peeled and
    chopped into ½-inch pieces
Olive oil
2 teaspoons sea salt
1 teaspoon freshly ground black
    pepper
½ cup chopped fresh parsley

TAHINI SAUCE

½ cup tahini
Juice of ½ lemon
1 to 2 garlic cloves (optional)
1 teaspoon sea salt
1 teaspoon freshly ground black
    pepper

Preheat the oven to 400°F and line two baking sheets with parchment paper.

Place the cauliflower on one prepared baking sheet and the carrot pieces on the other, drizzle both with olive oil, and sprinkle with the sea salt and pepper. Roast for 20 to 25 minutes until the vegetables are slightly browned.

Prepare the tahini sauce: Combine all the sauce ingredients in a blender with ½ cup of water and puree until smooth. Adjust the seasonings as you'd like.

Transfer the roasted cauliflower and carrots to a medium bowl and drizzle with the tahini sauce. Add the parsley and gently toss to combine.

The Sister A.G.T.O. Salad

Makes 4 servings

A.G.T.O. = avocado, goat cheese, tomato, and olive, an almost magical combination. This recipe is my sister's creation that I totally stole after realizing how much of a hit it was at every picnic and dinner party I brought it to. Fun additions could include grilled chicken, steak, or shrimp; quinoa; or garbanzo beans.

1 large or 2 small heads red leaf lettuce, washed and torn

3 Roma tomatoes, seeded and chopped

1 cup Kalamata olives, pitted and halved

2 grilled chicken breasts or other protein of your choice (optional)

1 avocado, peeled, pitted, and cubed

½ cup crumbled goat cheese

¼ to ½ cup Daily Basil Dressing (page 103)

Assemble the salad, adding the chicken, avocado, and cheese right before serving. Toss with the dressing to serve.

The Fall Salad You Won't Be Able to Quit

Makes 2 servings

It's not even an exaggeration. Have a busy week ahead? Make this salad. Not sure what to make? Make this salad. Have a party to take a dish to? Take this salad. The dressing and sweet potatoes can be prepped ahead of time for easy assembly. Add the avocado and cheese right before serving.

1 large or 2 small sweet potatoes or yams, chopped into ½-inch cubes

Olive oil

Sea salt

1 large or 2 small heads butter lettuce

1 small green apple, chopped into ½-inch cubes

½ avocado, peeled, pitted, and cubed

¼ cup chopped fresh herbs, such as chives, dill, and/or basil, plus more for garnish

Sprinkle of toasted pumpkin seeds (optional)

Crumbled goat cheese or feta (optional)

DRESSING

½ cup olive oil

2 to 3 tablespoons red wine vinegar

2 tablespoons Dijon mustard

1 cup fresh basil

1 tablespoon pure maple syrup

1 teaspoon sea salt

½ teaspoon freshly ground black pepper

Can be done ahead of time: Preheat the oven to 400°F and line a baking sheet with parchment paper. Toss the sweet potato with olive oil and sea salt and roast for 30 minutes, or until you can easily poke it with a fork. Remove from the oven and let cool.

Meanwhile, or when ready to serve, prepare the dressing: Blend together all the dressing ingredients.

To serve, place the cooled sweet potato and the rest of the salad ingredients in a serving bowl. Toss with the dressing and sprinkle with additional chopped fresh herbs.

Eating lunch is a radical act of self-care. And one that, more than any other meal, can dictate how the rest of your day goes, energy-, mood-, and hunger-wise.

Kale and Quinoa Salad with Squash, Apricots, and Bacon

Makes 6 to 8 servings

If delicata squash is not in season, use frozen precut butternut squash instead. Other fun additions could include goat cheese, avocado, pomegranate seeds, or hemp seeds sprinkled on top. This is a perfect make-ahead dish for busy weeks, delicious served warm or cold.

1 delicata squash

Olive oil

Sea salt

Freshly ground black pepper

1 cup uncooked quinoa

4 to 6 slices nitrate-free turkey bacon (optional)

2 heads leafy green or purple kale, stemmed and torn

½ cup dried apricots, chopped

¼ cup toasted pumpkin seeds (optional)

DRESSING

½ cup olive oil

2 tablespoons red wine vinegar

2 tablespoons Dijon mustard

1 tablespoon pure maple syrup

Sea salt

Freshly ground black pepper

Preheat the oven to 400°F and line a baking sheet with parchment paper.

Slice the delicata squash in half lengthwise, and scoop out and discard seeds. Slice into ¼-inch pieces and place on the prepared baking sheet. Drizzle the squash with olive oil, sprinkle with sea salt and pepper, and toss with your hands to coat. Roast for 20 to 25 minutes, stirring or rotating the pieces after the first 15 minutes.

Combine the quinoa and 2 cups of water in a small saucepan. Add a pinch each of sea salt and pepper, cover, and bring to a boil. Turn off the heat and let the quinoa cook, covered, for about 10 minutes, or until all the water is absorbed.

Meanwhile, heat a drizzle of olive oil in a large skillet over medium-high heat. When hot, add the bacon. Flip each strip halfway through cooking and remove when crisped. Set aside on a paper towel–lined plate.

Prepare the dressing: Whisk together all the dressing ingredients in a small bowl or mug, adding sea salt and pepper to taste; set aside.

Place the torn kale in a large serving bowl. Add the dressing and use your hands to rub each leaf until all are well coated. Crumble the bacon and add the quinoa, bacon, apricots, and roasted squash to the bowl. Gently toss to combine. Sprinkle with toasted pumpkin seeds to serve.

Thai Crab Cucumber Salad

Makes 2 servings

Green papayas are often found at specialty markets, but daikon radish makes a great and slightly spicy replacement that's more widely available. You'll need a box grater and julienne peeler, ideally, for this recipe—if you don't have one, a regular vegetable peeler can be a good backup. (See photograph on page 96.)

2 large daikon radishes,
 or 1 large green papaya

2 English cucumbers

½ cup cherry tomatoes, halved

½ cup chopped fresh basil,
 plus more for garnish

¼ cup chopped fresh parsley,
 plus more for garnish

¼ cup crushed roasted peanuts,
 plus more for garnish

4 ounces fresh cooked crab,
 shrimp, or chicken

Lime wedges for garnish
 (optional)

DRESSING

Juice of 1 lime

1 tablespoon Asian fish sauce

1 tablespoon pure maple syrup
 or honey

Sea salt

Freshly ground black pepper

Peel the daikon radishes or green papaya and the cucumbers. Grate the daikon or papaya with a large box grater, and julienne the cucumbers. Set both in a colander to let any excess water drain.

Prepare the dressing: Whisk together all the dressing ingredients in a small bowl, adding sea salt and pepper to taste.

Layer the daikon or papaya and cucumber into individual serving bowls, topping with the tomatoes, herbs, peanuts, and crab, if using. Drizzle with the dressing. Garnish with lime wedges and additional peanuts and herbs, if you wish.

Cozy Roasted Parsnip Soup

Makes 4 to 6 servings

This soup is so creamy and comforting, but so simple to make. If you can't find parsnips, use carrots or a large head of cauliflower in their place.

Olive oil

1 leek

1 large or 3 small parsnips (about 6 ounces)

2 russet potatoes or 6 small Yukon gold (about 6 ounces)

2 teaspoons sea salt

1 teaspoon freshly ground black pepper

4 cups organic chicken or vegetable stock

1 tablespoon grass-fed butter, ghee, or olive oil

Heat a bit of olive oil in a large stockpot over low heat. Cut off the top and bottom ends of the leek, and slice the stalk in half lengthwise so you have two equal pieces. Place each piece, cut side down, on a cutting board and slice thinly into equal-size pieces. Rinse in a colander to release any excess dirt. Pat dry. Add to the stockpot to caramelize.

Meanwhile, wash and peel the parsnips and potatoes, then chop into similarly sized pieces. When the leek has slightly browned, add the parsnips, potatoes, sea salt, pepper, and stock. Cover and bring to a boil, then lower heat to medium-low and cook for 10 to 15 minutes. Add the butter.

Transfer the soup to a blender and puree. Season with additional sea salt and pepper, if desired.

3-Ingredient Tomato Soup

Makes 2 to 4 servings

For how few ingredients this soup requires, the flavor is so delicious. Feel free to add your own additions as you have time, such as some extra garlic to the roasting process, some basil into the puree, or pulled chicken, organic sausage, or spinach to serve. For a more varied texture, blend half of the soup and leave the other half chunky.

8 Roma tomatoes, seeded and
    sliced
2 cups cherry tomatoes
2 leeks, sliced
Olive oil
Sea salt
Freshly ground black pepper
2 cups organic chicken stock

Preheat the oven to 400°F and line a baking sheet with parchment paper.

Place the Roma and cherry tomatoes and leeks on the prepared pan and toss with olive oil, then sprinkle with sea salt and pepper. Roast for 30 to 35 minutes, then remove from the oven and let cool slightly.

About 10 minutes before the tomatoes finish cooking, heat the chicken stock in a small sauce pan over medium heat.

Place the vegetables and stock in a blender and puree, adjusting the seasonings as needed. Serve warm.

Healthy Veggie Noodle Pho

Makes 2 to 4 servings

Pho is an ancient Vietnamese healing broth. This simplified recipe, inspired by traditional pho, is upgraded with a few extra veggies, anti-inflammatory spices, and zucchini noodles as the base. To enhance the flavor, you can add garlic, onion, or Asian fish sauce, or organic grilled chicken or beef, too.

Olive oil

3 carrots, chopped

1 jalapeño pepper, seeded and chopped

4 cups organic chicken or vegetable stock or bone broth

2 teaspoons ground turmeric

1 teaspoon ground ginger, or one (4-inch) piece fresh, grated

3 star anise pods

1 teaspoon sea salt

1 teaspoon freshly ground black pepper

2 large zucchini, spiralized into noodles, or brown rice or soba noodles

Handful of chopped fresh basil, parsley, and/or cilantro

Heat a bit of olive oil in a large stockpot over medium-high heat. Add the chopped carrots and jalapeño first, to brown. Pour in the stock and add the turmeric, ginger, star anise, sea salt, and pepper. Increase the heat to high and add the zucchini noodles. Cook for 1 to 3 minutes, until everything is warmed and noodles are cooked through. Serve hot, garnished with the herbs.

Roasted Kabocha Squash Soup

Makes 4 to 6 servings

There is something so decadent, delicious, and comforting about this soup, although the ingredients are so simple and clean. Fun toppings can include whole-milk Greek yogurt, crumbled rice crackers, avocado, chia or toasted pumpkin seeds, arugula, kale, shredded chicken, or pesto. If you can't find kabocha squash, use a large butternut squash, medium pumpkin, or any other variety you prefer in its place, equaling 2 to 3 cups when mashed. If you're short on time, you can skip the onion completely.

One 2- to 3-pound kabocha
　　squash
Olive oil
Sea salt
Freshly ground black pepper
½ onion, chopped
Two 13-ounce cans coconut milk
2 to 4 cups organic chicken
　　or vegetable stock
　　or bone broth

Preheat the oven to 425°F and line a baking sheet with parchment paper.

Place the squash whole on the prepared baking sheet, drizzle with olive oil, and sprinkle with sea salt and pepper. Roast for 45 to 50 minutes, or until you can easily poke it with a fork. Alternatively, if you have a great knife, you can cut the squash into pieces and scoop out the seeds before adding the olive oil and seasonings and baking, which may cut down on the overall roasting time. Both ways work great.

Remove the squash from the oven and let cool before you slice open, scoop out and discard the seeds, and place the flesh in a blender.

While the squash cools, heat the coconut milk and 2 cups of chicken stock in a medium saucepan over medium heat.

Meanwhile, heat a bit of olive oil in a large stockpot over medium-low heat. Add the onion and sauté for 5 minutes, or until translucent. Add the onion to the squash in the blender, along with the warm coconut milk and stock, 2 teaspoons sea salt, and 1 teaspoon pepper. Puree until smooth, adding more stock if you prefer a thinner consistency. Serve warm, with toppings of your choice, when ready to eat.

SNACKIES

Small Bites to Bridge the Gap

Supereasy Energy Balls   138

Coconut and Cocoa Nib Balls   141

Cinnamon Chocolate Energy Balls   142

Superfood Butter and Banana Bites   143

Vanilla Apricot Granola Bars   144

It's the intention of holding space for yourself that matters: a few minutes to tune in and gather up more goodness and energy to take into the rest of your day.

Supereasy Energy Balls

Each recipe makes 18 to 24 snack balls

Energy balls are my favorite in-between-meals snack, with beautiful amounts of healthy fats to keep you full and your blood sugar and energy stable. In my Spirulina Energy Balls, spirulina powder, which is packed full of B vitamins, iron, and protein, gives you an extra superfood boost at the time of day you need it most. For the days that you need a little midday pick-me-up, without a whole cup of matcha, try the Matcha Vanilla Energy Balls.

SPIRULINA ENERGY BALLS

6 tablespoons coconut butter

6 tablespoons coconut oil, melted

3 tablespoons cocoa nibs

2 tablespoons spirulina powder

2 tablespoons pure vanilla extract

1/4 cup small shredded unsweetened coconut flakes

COOKIE DOUGH ENERGY BALLS

1/4 cup coconut butter

1/4 cup mini chocolate chips

1/4 cup clean protein powder

3 tablespoons coconut oil, melted

3 tablespoons hemp seeds

1 tablespoon olive oil

1/4 teaspoon sea salt

Optional additions: peanut butter, chia seeds, coconut flakes

MATCHA VANILLA ENERGY BALLS

1/4 cup small shredded unsweetened coconut flakes

6 tablespoons coconut butter

1 tablespoon matcha powder

1/4 cup coconut oil, melted

2 tablespoons pure vanilla extract

1 tablespoon all-natural almond or peanut butter

1 tablespoon or more pure maple syrup or honey

1 tablespoon cocoa nibs

2 tablespoons pure vanilla extract

SNICKERDOODLE ENERGY BALLS

1/2 cup almond butter

3 tablespoons coconut flour

3 tablespoons almond, coconut, or hemp milk

2 tablespoons cinnamon, plus 1 tablespoon for rolling

1 tablespoon pure maple syrup

1 teaspoon pure vanilla extract

Combine all the ingredients for your chosen flavor in a bowl and mix well. For the Snickerdoodle Energy Bites, form into 18 balls, then roll in the extra cinnamon. For the other flavors, roll and form into 24 small balls. Store in the fridge until you're ready to eat. These keep great in a sealed container for up to six weeks, or longer in the freezer.

NOTE: To choose a clean protein powder, make sure you can read and recognize every ingredient (there should be 2 to 4 ingredients, max). I also have a few brands of clean and natural protein powder listed on the favorites page of my website, if you need an upgraded option.

Matcha Vanilla Energy Balls

RITUAL #6: FIND AFTERNOON JOYS

THE RITUAL: Create a pocket of time in your afternoon that adds a dose of joy and reenergizes your body to carry you through the rest of the day in a much more healthy and centered way.

When we were little, every day at around 3 or 4 p.m., we'd have what my mom called quiet time. It was a late afternoon break for her: to lie down or just rest for 15 to 20 minutes. My sister and I would follow her lead, or had the option to play or read quietly in our rooms. After quiet time, she'd put a kettle of hot water on the stove and we'd have tea: Earl Grey with a splash of cream for her, and mint with honey for us. We'd each get two small cookies, and sit at the table together for tea and cookie time.

Back then, we loved this: we got to drink tea like grown-ups, and we'd obviously take any excuse for a cookie. It was so calming, this little ritual my mom had, carried on from her own mother. But now, as an adult, I think the whole idea is just genius.

For most people, late afternoons are the time of day that everything tends to fall apart. Plans don't go the way they were supposed to, life throws something unexpected your way, or your willpower just naturally declines as the hours go on each day. All of which are just a part of real life, and therefore, things we can learn how to navigate better, instead of letting them take us down.

So, whether tea and cookies is something you take literally (so many healthier versions of both can be found here), or it's something you take in theory, it's the intention of holding space for yourself that matters: a timeout, a pause, and a few minutes to tune in to and gather up more goodness and energy to take into the rest of your day.

IDEAS FOR YOUR OWN AFTERNOON JOYS

- Teatime
- A walk
- A podcast or playlist
- A meditation
- Calling a friend
- Diffusing essential oils or rubbing them on your wrist
- Rose water face spray

Coconut and Cocoa Nib Balls

Makes 12 snack balls

A chocolaty little treat that packs a sneaky nutrient punch? Yes, please.

¼ cup coconut butter

1 teaspoon unsweetened cocoa powder

¼ cup macadamia nut butter or other nut butter of your choice

¼ cup small unsweetened coconut flakes

1 tablespoon pure vanilla extract

1 tablespoon pure maple syrup

1 tablespoon cocoa nibs

1 scoop collagen protein powder or protein powder of your choice, or flour of your choice

Warm the coconut butter in a small saucepan over low heat until it softens. Transfer to a small bowl. Add the cocoa powder first, then the rest of ingredients, and stir well to combine. Roll into 12 small balls and place in fridge for at least 1 hour. Store in fridge for up to six weeks.

Cinnamon Chocolate Energy Balls

Makes 24 snack balls

A little chocolate fix, without the sugar crash? Well, that's always a good idea in my book. Cinnamon is a natural blood sugar stabilizer, and cocoa powder is full of powerful antioxidants to make this a snack you can feel virtuous about eating, and in the hours that follow it.

½ cup shaved almonds

5 pitted Medjool dates

½ cup unsweetened coconut
  flakes

¼ cup coconut oil, melted

1 tablespoon unsweetened cocoa
  powder

2 tablespoons pure maple syrup,
  or more, to taste

1 teaspoon pure vanilla extract

½ teaspoon ground cinnamon
  (optional)

Place the shaved almonds in a blender and pulse until they crumble. Add the dates and pulse until combined. Transfer the mixture to a small bowl and add the rest of the ingredients. Stir well to combine. Taste and adjust the flavors as you'd like. Chill in the fridge for at least 10 minutes. Roll the mixture into 24 small balls, then store in the fridge or freezer until you're ready to eat.

Superfood Butter and Banana Bites

Makes 8 servings of nut butter or 6 to 8 banana bites

This amped-up nut butter is amazing on banana slices or banana chips, but it also pairs well with sliced apples or sprouted grain or gluten-free toast. My personal favorite? Straight from the fridge with a spoon if I'm on the run somewhere. Spirulina, a powerful superfood powder that helps with energy, detoxification, and cellular function, is also a perfect addition to your smoothies, bowls, and oatmeal.

1 teaspoon spirulina powder

2 tablespoons cocoa nibs

1/2 cup small unsweetened coconut flakes

1 teaspoon sea salt

1 cup almond butter, peanut butter, or nut butter of your choice

1 banana (optional)

If making superfood butter, mix together all the ingredients, except the banana, in a container with a lid, and enjoy on whatever vehicle you'd like.

If making banana bites, slice the banana into 1/2-inch pieces. On a small plate, heap the spirulina, cocoa nibs, coconut flakes, and sea salt in separate piles. Add a dab of nut butter to each piece of banana, then it dip into spirulina powder, and sprinkle with the cocoa nibs, coconut flakes, and sea salt.

Vanilla Apricot Granola Bars

Makes 8 to 10 bars or 12 to 16 snack bites

Because one look at the ingredients in most of the granola bars on the grocery shelf will have you running in the other direction, I love making a batch of these and keeping them wrapped in the fridge for an easy and much-better-for-you treat. Of course, you can use any dried fruit and nut combo that you like (or already have in your pantry). For the best texture, the trick is using two different kinds of dried fruit, at least two different kinds of nuts, and some sort of seeds. Chocolate chips or cocoa nibs would be a nice addition here, too.

½ cup honey

2 cups cashews

1 cup walnuts

½ cup pumpkin seeds

1 cup dried apricots

1 cup large unsweetened coconut
    flakes

½ cup dried cranberries

2 teaspoons pure vanilla extract

½ teaspoon sea salt

Melt the honey in a small saucepan over low heat. Meanwhile, chop the cashews, walnuts, pumpkin seeds, and apricots (roughly or finely—the texture is up to you). Combine all the ingredients in a medium bowl and mix well with a silicone spatula.

Line a medium square baking dish with parchment paper. Transfer the mixture to the prepared baking dish and press down evenly with the back of the spatula. Freeze for at least 1 hour, then remove from the dish to cut into bars. Store in the fridge until ready to eat.

EFFORTLESS EVENINGS

APERITIFING IS A VERB

Upgraded Apps and Snacks for
Having People Over

Socca Flatbread   151

Whipped Feta Dip   152

The Cutie Pink Hummus   155

Rosemary and Sea Salt Crackers   156

Garbanzo Bean Crunchies   158

Crispy Italian Chicken Wings   159

Bloody Mary Shrimp Cocktails   160

Chilled Cucumber Gazpacho   163

Just because you're eating healthier doesn't mean you're stuck with limp carrot sticks and bland hummus for the rest of your life. Here are a few upgraded and creative real-food apps and snacks for hosting.

HAVING PEOPLE OVER WITHOUT GOING CRAZY

- Create a signature house cocktail that people can assemble themselves or that you can make in batches. A few ideas? The Cucumber Mint Margarita (page 244), Mezcal Negroni (page 252), or Maple Old-Fashioned (page 256).
- Pick appetizers that are easy to make or prep ahead of time. Socca Flatbread (page 151), Whipped Feta Dip (page 152) with veggies, The Cutie Pink Hummus (page 155), or Bloody Mary Shrimp Cocktails (page 160) are perfect for this!
- Try picking a simple one-pot main meal, and adding a fun toppings bar that people can use to customize their meal. Try Roasted Sheet Pan Chicken and Veggies (page 176), Turkey Sausage and Veggie Polenta Bowls (page 190), or Cozy Sausage and Lentil Stew (page 169).

Socca Flatbread

Makes 4 servings

In southern France, *socca* is a traditional flatbread that happens to be naturally gluten-free because it's made with garbanzo bean flour. It's so good, and so easy to whip up anytime if you keep these basic staples in your house. You can use the base as a pizza crust, flatbread, or dipped in a fun sauce, such as Whipped Feta Dip (page 152) or the Cutie Pink Hummus (page 155) as an appetizer or side.

1 cup garbanzo bean flour

2 teaspoons sea salt, plus more for serving

1 teaspoon freshly ground black pepper

8 rosemary sprigs, chopped, or 1 tablespoon herbes de Provence

Olive oil, for pan

Combine all the ingredients, except the olive oil, in a medium bowl with 1 cup of warm water, stir well, then let sit for 30 minutes.

When ready to cook, preheat the oven to 450°F and heat a large cast-iron or ovenproof skillet over medium-high heat. Add a bit of olive oil to the pan as it heats. Pour the batter into the skillet and let cook for 2 to 3 minutes, until it begins to solidify. Transfer the skillet to the oven and bake for 3 to 4 minutes, then switch to BROIL for an additional minute. Cut into wedges and sprinkle with sea salt to serve.

Whipped Feta Dip

Makes 6 to 8 servings

The ultimate summer party app, this dip is make-ahead, and pairs well with any assortment of dippers: gluten-free crackers, olives, veggies, and so on. It also doubles as a topping or sauce for grilled meats, veggies, quinoa salads, or potatoes. This dip is best when made ahead and served chilled, if you have time. When ready to serve, drizzle a tiny bit of olive oil on top and sprinkle with extra chopped herbs.

8 ounces whole-milk feta

1 cup buttermilk or whole-milk yogurt

4 anchovy fillets, or 2 tablespoons anchovy paste

Juice of 1/2 lemon

1 teaspoon sea salt

1/2 teaspoon freshly ground black pepper

2 cups fresh parsley leaves, finely chopped, plus more for garnish

2 cups fresh cilantro leaves, finely chopped, plus more for garnish

1/2 cup fresh tarragon leaves, finely chopped, plus more for garnish

Olive oil for garnish (optional)

Place all the ingredients, except the herbs and olive oil, in a blender and blend. Transfer to a medium bowl and stir in the herbs. Let chill for at least 30 minutes before garnishing and serving with a drizzle of olive oil.

The Cutie Pink Hummus

Makes about 4 servings

This is such a beautiful showstopping little dish, and is so multifunctional. I love serving it with veggies and gluten-free crackers as a quick app, but it also does double duty as a Mediterranean-style salad dressing, an easy filling inside an avocado for lunch, or a spread in place of mayonnaise on anything (pink deviled eggs, anyone? Stop it). This hummus keeps well in the fridge for up to eight days, so have some fun using it on leftovers and whatever else you can dream up. It's great topped with extra sesame seeds (as pictured), toasted pumpkin seeds, or a chile-infused olive oil for a little spice. If you're short on time, use a clean store-bought hummus and puree in a blender with a cooked beet. Add extra seasonings, if desired.

⅓ cup olive oil, plus a splash for
    the onion
1 large sweet onion, thinly sliced
2 small cooked beets
Two 15-ounce cans garbanzo
    beans, drained and rinsed
4 garlic cloves
¼ cup freshly squeezed lemon
    juice
¼ cup tahini
2 teaspoons sea salt
1 teaspoon freshly ground black
    pepper
1 tablespoon sesame seeds for
    serving

Sauté the onion with a splash of olive oil in a skillet over medium heat until slightly browned. Transfer to a blender, add the beets, garbanzo beans, garlic, lemon juice, tahini, sea salt, and pepper, and puree until smooth, adding more olive oil or a bit of water if a thinner consistency is preferred. Season with sea salt and pepper, if desired, and sprinkle with sesame seeds to serve.

Rosemary and Sea Salt Crackers

Makes 24 to 30 small crackers

Other fun flavor combinations or add-ins for these gluten-free crackers include garlic, herbes de Provence, freshly ground black pepper, Parmesan, poppy seeds, chia seeds, or flaxseeds. Keeps fresh in a sealed container in the fridge for up to a week.

1 cup gluten-free flour

Leaves from 1 rosemary sprig, chopped

2 tablespoons olive oil

1 tablespoon grass-fed butter, melted

2 teaspoons honey

1 teaspoon sea salt

¼ teaspoon baking soda

Flaky sea salt for sprinkling (optional)

Preheat the oven to 400°F. Have a large baking sheet ready.

Combine all the ingredients, except the flaky sea salt, in a medium bowl with ½ cup of water and mix until smooth. Chill in the fridge for 5 minutes.

Place two sheets of parchment paper on the counter. Pour the batter onto the middle of one sheet of parchment. Cover the dough with the second piece of parchment. Using a rolling pin, roll out the dough until it's as thin as possible, without breaking. Lift away the top parchment sheet and place the bottom one and its batter on the baking sheet.

Bake for 15 minutes, or until slightly browned. Remove from the oven. Cut into small squares and flip each cracker over. Bake for another 5 to 7 minutes, until crackers are browned and crisp. Let cool fully before enjoying. Sprinkle with flaky sea salt to finish, if desired.

Garbanzo Bean Crunchies

Makes 2 or 3 servings

The ultimate crunch factor for salads, soups, or a quick and healthy snack: you can make these crunchy garbanzo beans hands-off style in the oven, or in a skillet for a crunchier result. I love both.

2 tablespoons olive oil,
   plus more for pan

Two 15-ounce cans garbanzo beans,
   drained, rinsed, and patted dry

2 teaspoons ground cumin

2 teaspoons herbes de Provence

1 teaspoon sea salt

½ teaspoon freshly ground black
   pepper

If using an oven, preheat to 450°F and line a baking sheet with parchment paper. If using a skillet, heat a big splash of olive oil in a large skillet over medium-high heat.

For either method, combine all the ingredients plus 2 tablespoons of olive oil in a large bowl and mix well. Spread on the prepared baking sheet and bake for about 10 minutes, or until slightly golden brown, or fry in the skillet until crispy.

Store in an airtight container in the fridge until ready to use.

Crispy Italian Chicken Wings

Makes 4 to 6 servings

When my husband, Kyle, and I first met, he didn't believe me when I said that there was a way to make almost every food into an upgraded real-food version. "Even chicken wings?" he said doubtfully. Five years later, one day, I looked over and these came off the grill at a party, with a big smile on his face and a crowd surrounding him, grabbing for a bite. You nailed it, babe, if I do say so myself.

3 pounds organic mini chicken wings

Juice of 1 lemon

¼ cup olive oil

3 tablespoons herbes de Provence

2 teaspoons sea salt

2 teaspoons freshly ground black pepper

Combine all the ingredients in a large resealable plastic bag or lidded container and let marinate for at least 1 hour, ideally.

Grill over high heat for 5 to 7 minutes per side, until cooked through. Serve hot.

Bloody Mary Shrimp Cocktails

Makes 2 to 4 servings

Serve cold in cocktail glasses, with any assortment of garnishes you choose: organic corn chips, pickled veggies, olives, avocado, jalapeño slices, celery stalks, or lime wedges. If you don't like shrimp, try using crab.

Olive oil

2 cups wild shrimp

Sea salt

Freshly ground black pepper

3 celery stalks, finely chopped

½ cucumber, peeled and cubed

1 cup peeled and cubed jicama

1 red bell pepper, seeded and
    chopped

½ red onion, finely chopped

Juice of 1 lime

½ cup vegetable juice

4 ounces tomato paste

2 dashes of hot sauce (optional)

Heat a drizzle of olive oil in a medium skillet over medium heat. When hot, add the shrimp and sprinkle with sea salt and pepper. Cook for 2 to 3 minutes, until seared, then flip. Cook for another 1 to 2 minutes, until the shrimp are opaque and cooked through.

Transfer the shrimp to a large bowl and add the remaining ingredients, including the hot sauce, if desired. Stir gently. Scoop the mixture into cocktail glasses and garnish with any of the items suggested above.

Chilled Cucumber Gazpacho

Makes 4 bowl servings or 24 shot glass servings for a party

This is an amazing party recipe (and/or perfect everyday recipe in the summer) served with grilled shrimp, cooked crab, or homemade gluten-free croutons on top. I highly suggest blending this recipe at least a few hours before serving, because the flavors meld together beautifully with some time. If your blender isn't a strong one, give the ingredients a rough chop before adding them.

2 English cucumbers, peeled, seeded, and roughly chopped

1 ½ cups green grapes

1 garlic clove

1 teaspoon white wine or red wine vinegar

¼ cup olive oil

1 teaspoon sea salt

½ teaspoon freshly ground black pepper

Place all of the ingredients in the blender with ½ cup of water and puree until smooth. Adjust the seasoning to taste. Serve chilled.

DINS TO WIN

Satisfying Meals for Any Night of the Week

Crustless Chicken Sausage and Veggie Pizza   167

Cozy Sausage and Lentil Stew   169

The Warm Shaved Brussels Sprout Caesar   171

Carrot Noodle Pad Thai   173

Grilled Shrimp and Kale Caesar Salad   174

Roasted Sheet Pan Chicken and Veggies   176

Coconut Green Curry Snapper Bowls   179

Broccoli Rice Paella   180

Smoked Salmon Pasta with Cashew Alfredo Sauce   183

Broccoli, Basil, and Goat Cheese Pizzas   184

Crispy Brown Butter Sole with Herby Green Rice   187

Spicy Chicken Burgers or Meatballs   188

Turkey Sausage and Veggie Polenta Bowls   190

Butternut Squash and Sage Risotto   193

Gigante Bean and Tomato Bake   194

Winter Greens Gratin   196

The Italian Situation   199

Sweet Potato Turkey Chili   200

Veggie Bowls with Coconut Lime Parsley Sauce   202

Poblano Chicken Tortilla Soup   205

I don't have time. I'm way too tired. *It's been a long day. I don't know what to make.* They're words I hear often. Dinner, as an afterthought. Dinner, as a last-minute panic. Dinner, as in the same four meals, every single week. Dinner, as one more thing on our already full to-do list.

One thing is for sure: a total revamp is necessary, both in the types ameals we make, and how we're thinking about the bigger and more magical role that dinner can play in our lives.

Crustless Chicken Sausage and Veggie Pizza

Makes 2 or 3 servings

Crustless pizza means all of the goodness and amazing flavor of everyone's favorite meal, but none of the heaviness that traditional versions can leave us with. It's my way of eating pizza, but upgraded in a way you can feel good about eating weekly. Feel free to use whatever pizza toppings and veggies you usually like here. I love adding olives, capers, and chopped anchovies to mine, with a little fresh arugula on top. The veggies and sausage can be cooked ahead of time to speed things up. You can add the cold cooked ingredients straight to the skillet and proceed with the recipe.

Olive oil

2 carrots, chopped

1 medium zucchini, cubed

1 bell pepper, seeded and chopped

1 pound organic ground Italian chicken sausage

One 32-ounce jar tomato sauce

One 8-ounce whole-milk mozzarella ball, torn into pieces, or 1 cup shredded Parmesan or mozzarella

Chopped fresh oregano or basil for garnish

Can be done ahead of time: Heat a bit of olive oil in a large, ovenproof skillet over medium-high heat. Add the veggies and cook until they begin to brown, about 15 minutes, then remove from the pan and set aside. Add a bit more olive oil to the pan and increase the heat slightly. Add the sausage, breaking up the pieces with a fork or spatula as you go.

Preheat the oven to 450°F.

When the sausage is browned, add the veggies back to the pan and evenly distribute them. Turn off the heat and cover everything with the tomato sauce.

Dot the mozzarella on the top and bake for 10 to 15 minutes, until the cheese melts. Then, broil for 1 to 2 minutes, until the cheese starts to brown. Remove from the oven and sprinkle with chopped oregano or basil to serve.

Cozy Sausage and Lentil Stew

Makes 6 to 8 servings

I love using French green lentils from the bulk section to make this soup—they hold their shape and texture much better than brown ones—but feel free to use whatever kind you have on hand. This stew is hearty and delicious, and can be made with or without the sausage. I love topping mine with arugula, avocado, or Parmesan. This recipe can also be made in a slow cooker if the sausage, onion, and garlic are cooked ahead of time. For a more traditional soup consistency instead of a stew, feel free to add more stock or water as you go.

Olive oil

1 pound organic ground turkey
   or chicken sausage

1 yellow onion, finely chopped

5 garlic cloves, finely chopped

4 to 5 carrots, chopped

4 to 6 celery stalks, chopped

2 cups dried French green lentils,
   rinsed

8 cups organic chicken
   or vegetable stock

1 tablespoon sea salt

2 teaspoons freshly ground black
   pepper

2 teaspoons cider vinegar or red
   wine vinegar

Heat a drizzle of olive oil in a large stockpot over medium-high heat. When hot, add the sausage and break up with a wooden spoon as it cooks. When meat is cooked through, remove the sausage from the pot and set aside. Add an additional drizzle of olive oil to the same pot, then add the onion and garlic and sauté over medium-low heat. When they begin to caramelize, increase the heat to medium, add the carrots and celery, and cook until browned.

Next, add the lentils, cooked sausage, stock, sea salt, pepper, and vinegar. Cover and bring to a boil, then lower the heat to medium and let the lentils cook for 25 to 30 minutes. Adjust the seasonings as desired and serve hot.

RITUAL #7: RECLAIM DINNER

THE RITUAL: Instead of thinking about dinner as a distraction or a chore, use it as a sacred time to relax, connect, and recharge. Because at its core, dinner is about human connection: to one another, to our food, and to ourselves. It's an act of feeding ourselves well, not only physically, but mentally and emotionally, too.

And when your food can stay simple and still delicious, you have more time and energy to focus on what really matters—the people around your table, and having time and space to be fully present with those you love.

Create nightly dinner rituals to keep things more lighthearted and fun. Some ideas:

- Mind-set check—repeat after me: "Cooking dinner more consistently is one of the best forms of self-care I can do for myself and others."
- Try a question bowl with fun questions for each person around the table to answer, or pick a theme for each day of the week and have everyone around the table chime in.
- Assign jobs to the people around your nightly dinner table: filling water glasses, setting the table, lighting candles, picking the playlist, peeling carrots, boiling water, heating up leftovers, mixing salad dressing, getting out condiments, and so on.
- Dining alone: A beautiful thing to behold—you get to call the shots, to pick exactly what you feel that your body needs the most. So, sit at the table. Light a candle. Pick your music. And know that feeding yourself well is a gift and an act of self-love and respect.

Prep your ingredients in batches, so your nightly routine becomes more about assembling what you've got instead of starting from scratch.

Keep it simple: one-pot or one-pan meals are always my go-to. Plus, there are fewer dishes to wash later. Dinner doesn't have to be fancy, or wildly different from night to night, unless you want it to be.

The Warm Shaved Brussels Sprout Caesar

Makes 2 servings

Growing up, I remember having intense stare-downs with the steamed whole Brussels sprouts sitting on my plate, doing whatever I could to avoid eating them. These days? I can't get enough. Thank goodness for better ways to cook this hearty vegetable so that it's actually enjoyable! In this recipe, Brussels sprouts get a fun upgrade as a salad base that's delicious served warm. You can add fresh herbs and Parmesan to serve, or pair with grilled chicken, shrimp, fish, or Garbanzo Bean Crunchies (000).

1 pound Brussels sprouts

Olive oil

Juice of ¼ lemon

2 teaspoons Dijon mustard

1 teaspoon anchovy paste

2 tablespoons olive oil

Shave the Brussels sprouts thinly with a mandoline or very sharp knife.

Heat a bit of olive oil in a medium skillet over medium high heat. Add the Brussels shreds and cook until they begin to brown.

Meanwhile, whisk the rest of the ingredients together in a small bowl. A minute before serving, drizzle on top of the sprouts so the mixture warms. Toss well to combine.

Carrot Noodle Pad Thai

Makes 2 servings

Instead of regular noodles, this recipe calls for carrot noodles, which gives it a beautiful color and texture and makes this a great guilt-free version of everyone's favorite Thai dish. Feel free to use brown rice or zucchini noodles in this recipe, if you prefer. You can easily turn leftovers into a soup by adding stock and coconut milk.

PAD THAI SAUCE

¼ cup natural almond
   or peanut butter
Juice of ½ lime
1 tablespoon tamari
1 tablespoon honey
1 teaspoon grated fresh turmeric,
   or ¼ teaspoon ground
1 teaspoon grated fresh ginger,
   or ¼ teaspoon ground
1 tablespoon olive oil

STIR FRY

Olive oil
10 carrots, spiralized into noodles
Sea salt
Freshly ground black pepper
¼ cup chopped fresh cilantro
¼ cup chopped fresh basil
½ lime, cut into wedges for
   serving

Prepare the sauce: Combine all the sauce ingredients in a saucepan over low heat with ¼ cup of water and stir occasionally until warm.

Heat the carrot noodles in a splash of olive oil in a large skillet over medium-high heat until they soften. Transfer the noodles to serving bowls and pour the warm sauce over them. Season with sea salt and pepper to taste, sprinkle with the cilantro and basil, and garnish with lime wedges to serve.

Grilled Shrimp and Kale Caesar Salad

Makes 4 servings

The shrimp in this recipe can be cooked ahead of time and served hot or cold. You can also use lentils, steak, or chicken. I also love this recipe with chopped romaine for a more traditional take. Whenever I make dressings, I always make extra for salads later in the week, so this recipe is written to make extra on purpose; feel free to halve the ingredients if you don't want leftovers. If you want to make it ahead of time, this salad gets better when it sits with light dressing on it for a day or two in the fridge; add the shrimp when you're ready to eat.

CAESAR DRESSING

½ cup olive oil

Juice of 1 lemon

2 teaspoons anchovy paste

2 teaspoons Dijon mustard

1 garlic clove (optional)

1 tablespoon Parmesan,
    plus more for garnish

1 teaspoon sea salt

1 teaspoon freshly ground black
    pepper

SALAD

Olive oil

8 wild shrimp

Sea salt

Freshly ground black pepper

1 large or 2 small bunches lacinato
    kale, stemmed and finely
    chopped

Prepare the dressing: Combine all the dressing ingredients in a blender and puree until smooth. Pour into a glass jar with a lid.

Heat a splash of olive oil in a large skillet over medium-high heat. Season the shrimp with sea salt and pepper and add to the skillet, searing completely on one side before flipping, 4 to 5 minutes per side.

In the meantime, place the chopped kale in a serving bowl and drizzle with the dressing. Toss to coat all the leaves well, then add the cooked shrimp on top. Sprinkle with extra Parmesan, if desired, to serve.

Roasted Sheet Pan Chicken and Veggies

Makes 4 servings

This is a true one-pan wonder and the most comforting, delicious meal to cozy up to in the fall or winter. It's ideal for having people over, or making on Sunday to have leftovers for the week.

4 bone-in organic chicken breasts or thighs

12 Brussels sprouts, halved

8 Yukon gold potatoes, quartered, or 1 cup baby potatoes, halved

5 carrots, chopped into 1-inch pieces

3 tablespoons olive oil

Leaves from 6 thyme sprigs

2 tablespoons herbes de Provence

2 teaspoons sea salt

2 teaspoons freshly ground black pepper

Preheat the oven to 450°F and line a large rimmed baking dish with parchment paper.

Place the chicken breasts in the prepared baking dish and scatter the veggies around the chicken. Drizzle everything with olive oil, sprinkle with the herbs, salt, and pepper, and rub in well to coat everything. Bake for 50 to 60 minutes, checking halfway through to rotate veggies, until the meat is cooked and juices run clear. Broil for the last 3 minutes to crisp and brown the chicken skin. Serve warm.

Coconut Green Curry Snapper Bowls

Makes 4 servings

Making curry at home seems fancy, but it really isn't as hard to do as most people think. In fact, it's one of my favorite ways to add tons of flavor to great basic meals, such as fish and veggies, with just a few pantry staples. Add a side of rice, quinoa, or potatoes to this dish, if you'd like.

Olive or coconut oil

4 carrots, peeled and chopped

2 cups cauliflower florets

1 bell pepper, seeded and chopped

1 cup snow peas or green beans, ends trimmed

1 teaspoon sea salt

1 teaspoon freshly ground black pepper

Four 4-ounce pieces wild snapper, or similar white fish

Handful of chopped fresh parsley for garnish

COCONUT CURRY SAUCE

One 13-ounce can coconut milk

2 tablespoons curry paste

2 teaspoons honey

Juice of 2 limes

2 teaspoons sea salt

2 teaspoons freshly ground black pepper

Heat a bit of olive or coconut oil in a large skillet over medium-high heat. Add the veggies and sauté until slightly browned, sprinkling with the sea salt and pepper halfway through.

In the meantime, prepare the sauce: Bring all the sauce ingredients to a simmer in a small saucepan until heated through. Set aside.

Remove the veggies from the pan and set aside. Add a bit more oil and increase the heat to high. When hot, add the snapper, cooking until the first side browns completely before flipping. Flip the fish and add back the veggies to warm.

Divide the veggies and fish among four serving bowls and spoon the sauce on top. Sprinkle with chopped parsley to serve.

Broccoli Rice Paella

Makes 4 to 6 servings

Broccoli rice can be purchased premade at most health food stores, or you can make your own with a food processor. Instead of the florets, broccoli rice makes use of the broccoli stems, leading to a milder flavor and less waste all around. You can also use regular rice in this recipe for a more traditional take on paella. But I love the idea of a comforting one-pot meal that feels decadent and rich, but is truly only made with vegetables and some protein. Talk about a guilt-free dinner that makes amazing leftovers for the week! Adding stock to this mixture later in the week would also turn leftovers into a delicious soup.

Olive oil
6 to 8 large wild shrimp
6 cups broccoli rice
   or 2 cups uncooked rice
1 cup cooked and shredded
   chicken breast
½ cup chopped fresh parsley
3 pinches saffron
1 teaspoon sea salt
1 teaspoon freshly ground black
   pepper

Heat a bit of olive oil in a large skillet over medium high heat. Add the shrimp first and cook, searing on both sides until done, about 5 minutes. Remove from the heat and set aside.

If using broccoli rice, lower the heat to medium, add another splash of olive oil, and add the broccoli rice and cook until slightly browned, stirring often. If using regular rice, place 4 cups of water in a medium saucepan and cook approximately 12 to 15 minutes until done. Add the chicken, shrimp, parsley, and spices to the skillet or saucepan and stir well to heat through and combine.

Smoked Salmon Pasta with Cashew Alfredo Sauce

Makes 2 servings

This fettuccine is naturally gluten-free and can be a completely dairy-free pasta dish if you use olive oil and omit the Parmesan. This is the definition of upgraded comfort food: it tastes amazing and decadent, but is made with just a few very simple and healthy ingredients. Feel free to swap out the smoked salmon for chicken or meat of your choice, or leave it out completely.

CASHEW ALFREDO SAUCE

½ cup cashews

1½ tablespoons grass-fed butter, ghee, or olive oil

½ cup chicken or vegetable stock

Juice of ¼ lemon

½ teaspoon gluten-free flour

Sea salt

Freshly ground black pepper

PASTA

2 cups uncooked brown rice pasta, or 4 to 6 zucchini, spiralized

1 head broccoli, broken into florets and roughly chopped

½ cup frozen peas

10 ounces wild smoked salmon

Chopped fresh parsley for garnish (optional)

Shredded Parmesan for garnish (optional)

Prepare the sauce: Place the cashews in a bowl of water to soak while you prepare the rest of the sauce. Melt the butter into the stock and lemon juice in a small saucepan over medium heat. Whisk in the flour, plus a sprinkling of sea salt and pepper. Remove from the heat. Drain the cashews and place them in a blender along with the warm sauce mixture. Blend on high speed for 1 minute, adding a bit of water if necessary. Set aside.

Bring a large pot of water and a medium pot of water to a boil. Add the noodles to the large pot and cook until al dente, according to the package instructions. Add the broccoli and peas to the medium pot and cook for 4 to 5 minutes, until they are bright green. Drain the water from both pots, leaving about 1 tablespoon of cooking water in the pasta pot.

Add the pasta back to the pasta pot along with the cooked vegetables. Drizzle with the Alfredo sauce and heat over medium-low heat. Tear or chop the smoked salmon into bite-size pieces and add to the pot. Stir everything together to mix well.

Garnish with chopped fresh parsley or shredded Parmesan, if desired.

Broccoli, Basil, and Goat Cheese Pizzas

Makes 4 servings

This is such a satisfying way to eat more veggies—because who doesn't love pizza? For the crust, I love using a simple frozen brown rice pizza crust (with just two ingredients) that you can buy at most health food stores, or a frozen cauliflower crust. I also adore these toppings sautéed on their own, minus the crust. If you are short on time, use an organic store-bought rotisserie chicken. Use the rest of your bunch of Swiss chard in your smoothies, an egg scramble, or a dinner skillet later in the week.

1 cup broccoli florets, chopped, if necessary, into bite-size pieces

Olive oil

Sea salt

Freshly ground black pepper

1 brown rice pizza crust or crust of your choice

2 Swiss chard leaves, stemmed and cut into thin ribbons

2 green onions, finely chopped

1 grilled chicken breast, cooked and shredded, or 1 cup shredded rotisserie chicken

¼ cup chopped fresh basil, plus more for garnish

Sprinkle of goat cheese, mozzarella, or Parmesan

CHARD PESTO

3 Swiss chard leaves, stemmed and roughly chopped

1 cup fresh basil

¼ cup olive oil

1 green onion, chopped

1 teaspoon sea salt

½ teaspoon freshly ground black pepper

Juice of ¼ lemon

Preheat the oven to 400°F. Line a baking sheet with parchment paper.

Place the broccoli florets on the prepared pan and toss with olive oil, sea salt, and pepper. Roast for 15 minutes, or until florets are slightly browned.

Meanwhile, prepare the chard pesto: Place all the pesto ingredients in a blender and blend until smooth.

Prebake the pizza crust according to the package instructions. Remove the crust from the oven and increase the oven temperature to 500°F. Add your pesto sauce, broccoli, chard, green onions, chicken, basil, and cheese to the pizza and place back in the oven. Bake until the crust starts to brown and the cheese softens. If you like a crunchier crush, broil for 1 to 2 minutes. Sprinkle with extra basil to serve.

Crispy Brown Butter Sole with Herby Green Rice

Makes 2 or 3 servings

This recipe is one of our favorites for dinner: it looks and feels fancy and oh so French, but is so quick and easy to throw together last minute. The rice can be made ahead of time, if desired.

1 large organic, cage-free egg

¼ cup coconut flour or gluten free flour blend

2 tablespoons herbes de Provence, plus more to garnish

1 teaspoon sea salt

1 teaspoon freshly ground black pepper

12 to 16 ounces wild sole fillets

2 tablespoons grass-fed butter

Herby Green Rice (recipe follows)

Heat a large skillet over high heat. In a large, shallow bowl, whisk the egg. In another large, shallow bowl, mix together the flour, herbes de Provence, sea salt, and pepper.

Working in batches, dip the fish in the egg mixture, then in the herbed flour, and fry on each side until browned, 2 to 3 minutes. Add the butter and heat until it melts. Serve hot with the herbed rice, sprinkled with extra herbes de Provence to garnish, if desired.

Herby Green Rice

Makes 4 servings

This is one of my favorite ways to use up leftover herbs and turn your pantry staple of plain rice into an impressive and superflavorful side dish for almost any meal.

Combine **3 cups organic chicken or vegetable stock** or water, **1½ cups rice**, and **1 teaspoon sea salt** in a stockpot, cover, and bring to a boil. Then, lower the heat to medium-low, cover, and let cook for 15 to 20 minutes, until all the liquid is absorbed. Add **2 tablespoons butter or ghee, 4 chopped green onions, 1 cup fresh basil (chopped), ½ cup chopped fresh parsley, 1 teaspoon sea salt**, and **½ teaspoon pepper**. Stir gently to combine and serve hot.

Spicy Chicken Burgers or Meatballs

Makes 4 small or 2 large burgers, or 6 to 8 meatballs

These flavor-packed burgers are delicious on their own, topped with my 1-Minute Miracle Sauce (recipe follows), Spicy Burger Sauce (recipe follows), clean ketchup, barbecue sauce, or a pineapple salsa, but are also a perfect addition added to lettuce wraps or gluten-free buns for a more classic take. For meatballs, just roll the mixture into 1-inch balls and fry over medium-high heat in a skillet, turning until each side browns.

1 pound organic ground chicken

5 canned chipotle chiles, drained, rinsed, and finely chopped

1 medium zucchini, shredded and excess water squeezed out

1 poblano pepper, finely chopped

Leaves from 5 oregano sprigs, finely chopped

¼ cup chopped fresh cilantro

2 teaspoons Dijon mustard

1 teaspoon sea salt

½ teaspoon freshly ground black pepper

Olive or coconut oil

LETTUCE WRAPS

1 head iceberg lettuce

1 medium zucchini or carrot, shredded (or whatever toppings you prefer)

½ avocado, peeled, pitted, and sliced

Lettuce wraps or gluten-free buns (optional)

1-Minute Miracle Sauce or Spicy Burger Sauce (recipes follow), or other condiments of choice

Combine all the burger ingredients, except the oil, in a large bowl and mix well.

Heat a drizzle of olive or coconut oil in a large skillet over medium-high heat. Form 2 large or 4 small burgers with your hands and add to the hot pan. Wait until the first side is browned completely before flipping, 5 to 7 minutes. Flip and cook the other side.

Assemble the burgers as desired.

1-Minute Miracle Sauce

Makes 2 to 3 servings

This sauce just makes everything better, and comes together with just a few pantry staples. Used as a salad dressing, burger sauce, dipping sauce for veggies, you name it, it works! I recommend making extra that you can store in the fridge for up to a week.

Whisk together **½ cup plain whole-milk Greek yogurt, ¼ cup chopped fresh herbs (dill, parsley, chives, basil, or tarragon), juice of ½ lemon,** and **sea salt** and **pepper** to taste in a small bowl until well combined.

Special Burger Sauce

Makes 2 servings

This sauce is an amazing addition to almost anything in the summer: burgers, chicken, quinoa, fish, veggies, and so on. To make it spicy, add a dash of hot sauce. Keeps in the fridge for up to a week.

Mix together **¼ cup Avocado Mayo** (page 109) or clean store-bought mayo, **2 to 3 table-spoons natural ketchup,** and **1 tablespoon relish or chopped pickle** in a small bowl until blended well.

Turkey Sausage and Veggie Polenta Bowls

Makes 4 servings

Okay, I know I'm not supposed to pick favorites, but this dish just might be my favorite cozy meal of all time. I can't even count the times I have made or brought this dish to friends and family, when a hug in a bowl is needed. Even the pickiest eaters have been known to lick the plates.

1½ pounds organic ground turkey sausage

6 carrots, quartered and chopped

2 red bell peppers, seeded and chopped

2 medium zucchini, quartered and chopped

2 teaspoons sea salt

2 teaspoons freshly ground black pepper, or to taste

1 bunch kale, torn or chopped into bite-size pieces

Herby Parmesan Polenta (recipe follows)

Cook the sausage first in a large stockpot over medium-high heat, browning it on all sides. Next, add the carrots and let cook for 5 to 7 minutes, then add the bell peppers and zucchini. Season with the sea salt and pepper. Add the kale and cook for 2 to 3 minutes, until wilted.

Meanwhile, make the Herby Parmesan Polenta. When the polenta is ready, scoop into individual bowls to serve hot, topped with the sausage and veggie mixture and garnished with extra Parmesan.

Herby Parmesan Polenta

Bring **4½ cups stock** or water to a boil in a saucepan with a lid. Add **1 cup polenta (corn grits), 1 tablespoon herbes de Provence,** and **1 teaspoon sea salt** and cook for about 10 minutes, or until all the liquid is absorbed.

Add **2 large pats butter or ghee** and **¼ cup shredded Parmesan** and let melt. Garnish with extra Parmesan, if desired.

Butternut Squash and Sage Risotto

Makes 2 servings

This is a lighter, veggie-style risotto for cozy nights. It couldn't be easier to make, and it's guilt-free, too.

Olive oil

2 cups peeled, seeded, and cubed butternut squash

1½ cups uncooked rice

1 teaspoon sea salt, plus a pinch to cook rice

2 cups spinach or chopped kale

1 cup organic chicken or vegetable stock

2 cups shredded Gruyère or Parmesan (optional)

¼ cup chopped fresh parsley, plus more for garnish

2 tablespoons dried sage, or 12 fresh leaves, chopped

1 teaspoon freshly ground black pepper

Heat a bit of olive oil in a large skillet over high heat. Add the squash cubes and cook until browned on all sides.

Meanwhile, combine 3 cups of water with the rice and a generous pinch of sea salt in a stockpot. Bring to a boil, then cover, lower the heat to a simmer, and cook until the rice absorbs all the water, 10 to 15 minutes.

Add the spinach to the squash and sauté until it begins to wilt, 1 to 2 minutes. When rice is done, add it to the skillet along with the stock, the cheese, if using, and the parsley and sage.

Stir until the cheese melts, the stock is absorbed, and the mixture is well combined. Season with the remaining salt and the black pepper and garnish with chopped parsley.

Gigante Bean and Tomato Bake

Makes 8 servings

Gigante beans, a.k.a. Italian beans, are much larger than other white varieties and have a smooth creamy texture. They're most commonly found in the bulk food section at natural food stores, or can be ordered online. They're such a helpful staple to have in your pantry and add to your rotation because they're so versatile and meaty. If you can't find them, dried great northern or cannellini beans can be used in their place. For this recipe, be sure to soak and cook the gigante beans ahead of time to speed up the process.

4 cups dried gigante beans

2 teaspoons sea salt

One 32-ounce jar tomato sauce

One 8-ounce ball mozzarella, sliced

1 teaspoon freshly ground black pepper

½ cup chopped fresh basil

8+ hours before you're ready to cook: Cover the beans with at least 3 inches of water in a bowl or large pot and let soak for at least 8 hours, and up to 48 hours, before.

When ready to cook, drain and rinse the beans from the soaking water and place in a stockpot along with the sea salt. Cover with 2 inches of fresh water or stock (about 8 cups). Cover the pot and bring to a boil, then lower the heat to medium-low and let cook for 1 hour, or until the beans are soft and can be easily poked with a fork. Drain, rinse, and set aside.

Preheat the oven to 450°F. Place the cooked beans and tomato sauce in a large, ovenproof skillet or casserole dish. Toss well to combine. Dot the mozzarella on top, bake for 5 to 7 minutes, then broil for 1 to 2 minutes, until the cheese begins to bubble and brown. Garnish with the chopped basil and serve hot.

Winter Greens Gratin

Makes 6 to 8 servings

This cozy one-pot meal is always a crowd-pleaser (and a sneaky and delicious way to add more nutrient-dense dark leafy greens to your life). This dish is perfect for having people over or bringing to a potluck, as it can be made ahead of time and tastes great served warm or at room temperature.

Olive oil

1 pound organic Italian sausage

6 bunches (about 3 pounds) collard greens, kale, or Swiss chard, stemmed and sliced into ribbons

1 cup organic chicken or vegetable stock

3 tablespoons almond, brown rice, or gluten-free flour

2 teaspoons sea salt

1 teaspoon freshly ground black pepper

1 tablespoon grass-fed butter, ghee, or olive oil

¼ cup heavy cream

¼ cup grated Parmesan

Preheat the oven to 375°F and oil an 8-by-12-inch casserole or gratin dish with olive oil and set aside.

Brown the sausage in a large stockpot over medium heat until cooked through, breaking up with a wooden spoon as you go. Remove the sausage from the pot and set aside. In the same pot, heat an extra drizzle of olive oil, then add the greens in bunches until they wilt and cook down.

Add the stock and cover the stockpot for 5 to 10 minutes, until all the liquid is absorbed. Drain away any excess liquid if it does not evaporate. Add the flour, sausage, salt, and pepper to the greens and stir well to combine. Transfer the mixture into the prepared baking dish, dot with pieces of butter, pour the cream on top, and sprinkle with the cheese. Cover and bake for 30 minutes.

Remove the cover and broil for 1 to 2 minutes for a golden brown, bubbling crust.

RITUAL #8: SIMPLIFY YOUR WEEKENDS

THE RITUAL: Follow these easy steps to simplify your weekends.

1. Keep up with your nonnegotiables: eating veggies, drinking water, having a real lunch, and eating when you are actually hungry.

2. Make a one-pot or make-ahead recipe on Thursday or Friday, for an easy weekend meal option that's ready to go.

3. Stick to a somewhat similar eating rhythm to your weekdays. A.k.a. don't snack all day or pick at random food just because you have more flexibility in your schedule. This is called boredom, not hunger. If it strikes often, this may be a great sign to start finding other activities that can bring more fun and joy into your life, so all the pressure doesn't end up on food alone.

4. Pick the occasions and foods that matter and mean the most to you.

The Italian Situation

Makes 8 servings

This thick, all-veggie stew is one of my all-time favorites to make ahead for busy weeks. It's warm and comforting, but packed with nutrient-dense vegetables to keep your body energized and running strong. Serve with crushed rice crackers or sliced avocado on top, if desired.

Olive oil

7 carrots, peeled and chopped

5 cups chopped broccoli florets

5 to 6 cups broccoli rice

Two 28-ounce cans crushed
  tomatoes

4 cups stock

1 cup uncooked white rice

2 teaspoons sea salt, plus more for
  serving

2 teaspoons freshly ground black
  pepper

½ bunch parsley, roughly
  chopped

Grated Parmesan for garnish
  (optional)

Heat a bit of olive oil in a large stockpot over medium heat, then add the carrots and cook until browned. Add the broccoli florets and cook until softened. Remove the carrots and broccoli from the pot and set aside. Add the broccoli rice in the same pot and cook for 7 to 10 minutes, until browned. Return the carrots and broccoli to the pot and add the tomatoes, stock, rice, sea salt, and pepper.

Cover and bring to a boil, then lower the heat to a simmer and cook for 10 to 15 minutes, until the soup is thickened as the rice expands. Turn off the heat and let sit covered for 5 minutes before serving. Garnish with chopped parsley, extra sea salt and pepper, or Parmesan, if desired.

Sweet Potato Turkey Chili

Makes 4 to 6 servings

This soup is also a good option for a slow cooker—just brown the onion and meat before adding the other ingredients and cook on HIGH for four hours or LOW for six. Or, if making traditionally, follow the instructions below. Great additions to the soup include cooked quinoa, avocado, whole-milk sour cream, cheese, lime wedges, green onions, or organic tortilla chips. To make this as a vegetarian dish, just leave out the meat. This is also a perfect one for a crowd, served with a toppings bar.

Olive oil

½ yellow onion, chopped

8 ounces organic ground turkey, chicken, or beef

3 carrots, chopped

1 small yam or sweet potato, peeled and chopped

5 to 6 celery stalks, chopped

One 15-ounce can baked beans, top liquid drained off (look for baked beans without corn syrup)

1 red bell pepper, seeded and chopped

One 28-ounce can whole peeled tomatoes

2 cups organic chicken stock

1 teaspoon sea salt

1 teaspoon freshly ground black pepper

½ teaspoon ground cumin

½ teaspoon chili powder

½ teaspoon dried oregano

Heat a large heavy pot over medium heat with a splash of olive oil. Add the onion and sauté until translucent. Remove the onion from the pot, increase the heat to medium-high, and add the ground turkey. Cook until browned, then add all the other ingredients to the pot and let cook together for 5 to 7 minutes. When ready to serve, scoop into bowls and add any extra toppings you'd like.

Veggie Bowls with Coconut Lime Parsley Sauce

Makes 4 servings

Never made buckwheat? It's worth giving a try. It has a tasty flavor and chewy rice-like texture, and cooks just as fast as quinoa, at around 10 minutes. Find it in the bulk or grain section of your natural food store, or use organic white rice, quinoa, or your favorite gluten-free grain instead. This dish also makes an easy savory breakfast on the go if you divide it among a few glass storage containers or individual mason jars to let the sauce absorb. Add grilled chicken, steak, shrimp, or avocado on top, if desired. You can also use any leftover roasted, grilled, or sautéed veggies.

The Coconut Lime Parsley Sauce is amazing on almost everything. Try it on any grilled fish, meat, potatoes, grains, or veggies. You can also make it ahead; the sauce keeps in the fridge for up to eight days.

1 teaspoon sea salt, plus more for buckwheat and veggies

1 cup uncooked buckwheat groats, or other gluten-free whole grain of your choice

Olive oil

1 teaspoon freshly ground black pepper, plus more for veggies

4 carrots, sliced into rounds

1 bell pepper, seeded and thinly sliced

4 baby bok choy, halved

2 small zucchini, thinly sliced

1 cup snow peas

Place 2 cups of water, the sea salt, and the buckwheat groats in a medium saucepan. Cover and bring to a boil. Then, lower the heat to a simmer and cook for 10 minutes, or until the water absorbs. Remove from the heat and set aside.

Meanwhile, heat a bit of olive oil with some sea salt and pepper in a large skillet. Add and cook, in the following order, the carrots, bell pepper, bok choy, zucchini, and snow peas until warm but still crunchy.

Meanwhile, prepare the sauce (see ingredients on page 203): Heat a splash of olive oil in a separate medium saucepan over medium heat. Add the shallot and ginger and cook until golden brown. Then, add the coconut milk, lime juice, lemon juice, the chopped herbs, and the sea salt and pepper and quickly whisk. Remove from the heat and leave as is, or blend everything together in a blender.

Divide the cooked buckwheat among individual serving bowls, add the veggies on top, and pour the sauce over all. Serve warm. Garnish with additional chopped cilantro and parsley, if desired.

COCONUT LIME PARSLEY SAUCE

Olive oil

1 large shallot, sliced

One 2-inch piece fresh ginger, finely
    chopped or grated

6 ounces canned coconut milk

Juice of ½ lemon

Juice of 1 lime

Leaves from 1 bunch parsley, roughly
    chopped, some reserved for garnish

Leaves from 1 bunch cilantro, roughly
    chopped, some reserved for garnish

1 teaspoon sea salt

½ teaspoon freshly ground black
    pepper

Poblano Chicken Tortilla Soup

Makes 4 servings

This soup is awesome served with a fun toppings bar of chopped green onions, black or pinto beans, lime wedges, organic tortilla chips, or avocado. Don't worry about precise chopping as you prepare it, because it's all getting blended anyway. If you are short on time, use store-bought organic rotisserie chicken.

1 to 2 raw chicken breasts, or breast meat from a rotisserie chicken

Olive oil

1 medium sweet onion, roughly chopped

4 garlic cloves, roughly chopped

1 poblano pepper, chopped

1 jalapeño pepper, chopped (optional)

Two 28-ounce cans crushed tomatoes

2 tablespoons grass-fed butter or ghee

4 cups organic chicken or vegetable stock

Generous sprinkle of sea salt

Generous sprinkle of freshly ground black pepper

If you are cooking your own chicken, bring a small pot of water to a boil, add the chicken breasts, cover, and lower the heat to medium-low. Cook for 10 minutes, or until cooked through, discard the water, and shred the meat with a fork. Alternatively, you can bake the chicken.

Heat a drizzle of olive oil in a large stockpot over medium-low heat. Add the chopped onion and garlic and caramelize for 5 minutes, then add the poblano and jalapeño peppers (if using) and cook until softened, about 5 minutes.

After the peppers have browned in the stockpot, add the tomatoes, butter, stock, sea salt, and pepper. Cook for 2 to 4 minutes to warm the stock. Transfer the mixture to a blender and puree until creamy. Add the shredded chicken and any desired toppings right before serving.

SIDESHOWS
Pairings for Any Meal

The Green Bean Dream   209

The Husband Fries   210

Herby Roasted Corn Salad   213

Green Bean, Cantaloupe, and Basil Salad   214

Grilled Broccoli and Avocado with Sesame Seeds   216

Tomato Salad with Feta and Pistachios   218

Showstopping sides to
complement any meal.

The Green Bean Dream

Makes 4 servings

These green beans pair perfectly with salmon, shrimp, steak, or potatoes. They are also amazing as a make-ahead picnic-style salad, served hot, at room temperature, or cold.

Olive oil

1 red onion, thinly sliced

1 pound organic green beans, ends trimmed

1 tablespoon garlic-infused olive oil, or 1 garlic clove grated into 1 tablespoon olive oil

1 cup fresh cilantro, finely chopped

Zest of 1 lemon

1 teaspoon sea salt

½ teaspoon freshly ground black pepper

Sprinkle of feta, goat cheese, or grated Parmesan (optional)

Heat a bit of olive oil in a skillet over low heat. Add the red onion and cook, stirring as needed, for 5 to 7 minutes, until caramelized.

Meanwhile, bring a pot of water to a boil (heat enough water to cover the green beans). Then, add the beans and let cook for 1 to 2 minutes, until they turn bright green. Drain the beans in a colander and rinse immediately with cold water. Transfer the green beans to a serving dish.

Drizzle the beans with the garlic-infused olive oil. Add the caramelized onion on top, then sprinkle with the cilantro, lemon zest, sea salt, pepper, and cheese, if using.

The Husband Fries

Makes 4 servings

These are Kyle's "house specialty." As in, I am not allowed even near the oven when these go down . . . which is at least once a week in our house, and often when people come over. I love these dipped in natural ketchup or Dijon mustard.

2 russet potatoes

Olive oil

1 teaspoon sea salt

1 teaspoon freshly ground black
    pepper

2 teaspoons herbes de Provence

Preheat the oven to 450°F and line a baking sheet with parchment paper.

Slice the potatoes into thin wedges of similar thickness. Place them all on the prepared baking sheet and drizzle with olive oil. Rub each wedge thoroughly with your hands to coat well, then space out evenly on the pan. Sprinkle with the sea salt, pepper, and herbs and roast for 15 minutes. Remove from the oven and flip the potatoes. Roast for 10 to 15 minutes more, or until browned and crispy.

Herby Roasted Corn Salad

Makes 6 servings

Using fresh organic corn in the summer will give you the best results with this salad. It's amazing on its own, or as topping on burgers, fish, tacos, mixed into green salads, or with added chicken or steak as a make-ahead deli-style dish. If you love a little heat, keep the chipotle pepper seeds intact. If you prefer a milder heat, remove the seeds. This dish keeps well in the fridge for three or four days (without the cheese).

6 ears organic corn, husks removed

Olive oil

1 cup fresh cilantro, finely chopped

3 green onions, finely chopped

10 to 12 chive stalks, finely chopped

2 chipotle chiles in adobo sauce, chopped

Juice of 4 limes

Sea salt

Freshly ground black pepper

Sprinkle of feta (optional)

Preheat the oven to 400°F. Rub the ears of corn with olive oil and roast for 15 to 20 minutes, until they start to brown. Remove from the oven and let cool, then slice the kernels off the cobs and place in a large mixing bowl, along with the cilantro, green onions, chives, and chipotles. Add the lime juice, 1 tablespoon olive oil, salt, and pepper to taste as you gently mix the salad together. Sprinkle with feta, if using, before serving.

Green Bean, Cantaloupe, and Basil Salad

Makes 4 to 6 servings

This side dish can keep fresh in the fridge for one to two days, and is a fun and colorful option to bring to any party. It's also excellent over fresh spinach or butter lettuce; with added grilled salmon, fish, chicken, or steak; or with fresh blueberries.

2 cups green beans, ends trimmed

2 cups cherry tomatoes, halved

½ cantaloupe, scooped with a melon baller

½ cup chopped fresh basil

1 cup small mozzarella balls

Sprinkle of sea salt

Sprinkle of freshly ground black pepper

DRESSING

2 tablespoons red wine vinegar

¼ cup olive oil

2 teaspoons Dijon mustard

Sea salt

Freshly ground black pepper

Bring a large pot of water to a boil and add the green beans. Cover and cook for 2 minutes, then quickly drain, rinse with cold water, and set aside.

Prepare the dressing: Whisk together the dressing ingredients in a small bowl, adding salt and pepper to taste.

Place the green beans, tomatoes, cantaloupe, basil, and mozzarella, in a bowl or on a serving platter. Drizzle the dressing on top and sprinkle with sea salt and pepper to serve.

Grilled Broccoli and Avocado with Sesame Seeds

Makes 4 servings

Never grilled an avocado? You are missing out in life. Try it in other salads, too.

2 heads broccoli, halved lengthwise so
    the stalks lay flat, or broccolini
2 avocados, halved and pitted
3 tablespoons garlic-infused olive oil,
    or 1 garlic clove grated into
    3 tablespoons olive oil
Sea salt
Freshly ground black pepper
2 tablespoons sesame seeds
3 tablespoons toasted sesame oil

Preheat a grill to high heat.

Place the broccoli and avocado halves in a medium bowl, top with the garlic-infused olive oil, and sea salt and pepper to taste, and rub in to coat each surface well. Place the broccoli on the grill first and cook for 5 to 7 minutes. until slightly crispy.

After 5 minutes place the avocados, face down, on the grill to quickly char. Remove when they get grill marks, 1 to 3 minutes, and transfer to a platter along with the broccoli. You can slice the avocado into crescent moon shapes, or leave in their skin to serve. Sprinkle everything with sesame seeds and additional sea salt and pepper, and drizzle with toasted sesame oil.

RITUAL #9: SPICE UP YOUR SEASONS

THE RITUAL: Each of the four seasons throughout the year has a different energy and rhythm to it. New foods ripen as others hibernate, and learning how to do the same with our body, routines, and foods is such a beautiful practice to start to embrace. Plus, it keeps things fresh and exciting: getting stuck in a rut or bored with eating the same food every day is one of the biggest reasons people get off track—as humans, we love newness and excitement.

Here are some tips to get seasonal:

1. Try new recipes: Pick five new recipes each season that embrace that season's energy, and keep them on rotation until you know them by heart and feel confident enough to make them on your own.

2. Upgrade your annual seasonal traditions: Food plays such a big role in how we celebrate almost every occasion in life. Birthdays have cakes, the Fourth of July means barbecues and burgers, and Thanksgiving is usually defined by mashed potatoes and turkey.

Instead of falling into autopilot, sit down at the beginning of each season and take a look at the upcoming holidays and celebrations. Think about what food traditions you love best, so you can upgrade those classic recipes with real-food ingredients, or try out some entirely new ones. Just because it's what you've always done or made, doesn't mean it makes you feel good. Reinventing old traditions with better food is a powerful legacy to leave.

3. Embrace seasonal activities: Make a bucket list of fun seasonal self-care activities that you want to incorporate, to fully embrace each shift in the year.

Tomato Salad with Feta and Pistachios

Makes 2 servings

Assemble this salad right before serving, for best results. I like to layer the tomatoes first, then add the cheese, then sprinkle with arugula, like a reverse salad. Serve on its own or with toasted gluten-free bread as a great appetizer or part of meze night, or add grilled chicken, fish, lamb, or steak, and a big green salad, which can easily make this an entire meal.

3 to 4 heirloom tomatoes, sliced

2 cups arugula

1 cup sliced cherry tomatoes

½ cup crumbled feta or whole-milk ricotta

⅓ cup chopped pistachios

Drizzle of olive oil

Generous sprinkle of sea salt

Generous sprinkle of freshly ground black pepper

Layer the heirloom tomatoes, arugula, cherry tomatoes, cheese, and pistachios together on a platter or serving dish. Drizzle with olive oil and sprinkle with sea salt and pepper to serve.

SWEETS
AND SIPS

SWEETS
Guilt-Free Recipes to Savor the Fun Parts of Life

Flourless Everything Cookies 224

Salted Dark Chocolate Peanut Butter Cups 226

Mint Chocolate Coconut Milkshakes 227

Healthy Maple Graham Crackers 228

Flourless Brownies 231

Healthy Crispy Rice Bars 232

Chocolate Chip Olive Oil Cookies 235

Flourless Chocolate Crinkle Cookies 236

Ice-Cream Sandwiches 239

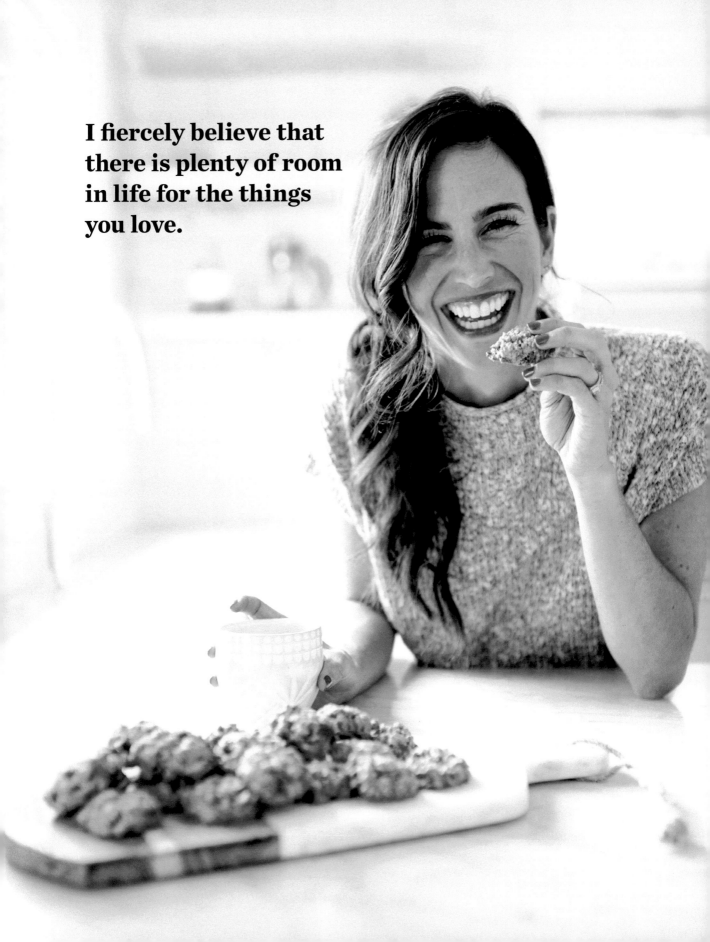

I fiercely believe that there is plenty of room in life for the things you love.

Flourless Everything Cookies

Makes about 24 small cookies or 12 medium ones

I love a good cookie—it's one of my all-time favorite treats. And this version has it all, without any flour added to it, making it full of hearty nutrients and texture. You can even get away with these as a breakfast treat, because they have eggs, coconut oil, nut butter, and chia and flaxseeds, which give these cookies a good amount of healthy fat and protein to keep your blood sugar stable afterward. Either way, they taste amazing and are always in heavy rotation in our weekend kitchen.

2 cups gluten-free oats

2 large organic, cage-free eggs

1 cup unbleached cane
    or coconut sugar

1 cup unsweetened coconut flakes

½ cup coconut oil, melted

½ cup raisins

½ cup chopped dark
    or unsweetened chocolate

½ cup peanut butter
    or other nut butter

½ cup chopped walnuts
    (optional)

1 tablespoon flax- or chia seeds
    (optional)

2 teaspoons pure vanilla extract

Sea salt for sprinkling

Preheat the oven to 350°F and line two baking sheets with parchment paper.

Combine all the ingredients, except the sea salt, in a large bowl and mix well. Form the batter into two dozen 1-inch balls, space apart evenly on the prepared baking sheets, and bake for 10 to 15 minutes, or form one dozen 2-inch balls and bake for 30 minutes, or until done to your liking. Sprinkle with sea salt before serving.

RITUAL #10: DEFINE YOUR LOVES

THE RITUAL: This ritual is a simple one:

1. Define your loves, SPECIFICALLY. Specificity is important.

2. Get rid of the rest. A.k.a. the clutter. If you don't 100 percent, absolutely, positively LOVE it, stop wasting your life and time on it.

A glass of wine, a great cocktail, a fresh piece of homemade sourdough bread with butter, dark chocolate, and sea salt? Yes, please. The trick is to be very clear on what those things are for you. For most people, there are usually only two or three things that truly light you up, make life worth living, and bring you so much joy when you have it. And as long as you upgrade the ingredients to the highest quality you can find, or learn how to make your own cleaner versions at home, there should be no guilt in having and enjoying these things in your life from time to time.

Salted Dark Chocolate Peanut Butter Cups

Makes 12 servings

That's right. No need for the packaged versions ever again with these three- (real) ingredient wonders! You'll need a mini muffin tin and liners for the best results. Keep in the fridge until ready to eat. Also great stored in the freezer.

18 ounces dark chocolate, or six 3-ounce dark chocolate bars
One 18-ounce jar natural peanut butter
Sprinkle of flaky sea salt

Melt the chocolate in a saucepan over medium heat. Line 12 wells of a mini muffin tin with paper liners. Pour or scoop the chocolate into the prepared wells to fill each halfway and then chill in the fridge for at least 15 minutes, or until the chocolate cools and hardens.

Next, melt the peanut butter over very low heat until it softens slightly. Remove the muffin tin from the fridge and spoon tiny bits of melted peanut butter over the chocolate, then sprinkle with flaky sea salt. Chill in the fridge for at least 30 minutes before eating.

Mint Chocolate Coconut Milkshakes

Makes 2 servings

Because an easy upgraded milkshake is just a good life skill to have! Other fun twists on this recipe include using frozen fruit, homemade cookies, or natural M&M's instead of the chocolate bar.

2 cups coconut milk ice cream
1 ounce dark mint chocolate,
    finely chopped
1 cup coconut milk

Place all the ingredients in a blender and blend on low speed until combined. Scoop out into glasses and serve with a fun straw or spoon.

Healthy Maple Graham Crackers

Makes 2 to 3 dozen mini crackers

A little four-ingredient sweet treat in under 20 minutes? Yes, please. Everyone's childhood favorite snack just got upgraded.

2 cups almond meal

1 cup pure maple syrup

2 teaspoons ground cinnamon

2 teaspoons baking powder

Preheat the oven to 375°F.

Mix together all the ingredients in a medium bowl.

Cut two pieces of parchment paper to the size of a baking sheet. Place the first piece of parchment on the counter. Pour the batter onto the middle of the parchment paper. Cover the batter with another piece of parchment paper and a rolling pin to flatten the batter evenly, to about ¼ inch thick all the way around.

Remove the top parchment sheet and place the bottom sheet and dough on the baking sheet. Bake for 15 to 20 minutes, or until the crackers solidify. Remove from the oven and cut into 2 to 3 dozen mini crackers, flipping each over. Place back in the oven to bake for 3 to 5 minutes, until crisp. Remove from the oven and let cool before enjoying.

THE SCALE OF SUGARS

Ranked by speed of release to blood sugar: slowest to fastest

Fruit

Dried fruit (dates, apricots, figs, goji berries, apples, pineapples)

Honey, pure maple syrup, blackstrap molasses

Organic coconut sugar

Organic demerara sugar

Organic cane sugar

Sweeteners to Avoid: stevia, agave, monkfruit, artificial sweeteners, high-fructose corn syrup

Flourless Brownies

Makes 9 to 12 bars

Feel free to add a drop of peppermint extract, cocoa nibs, chocolate chips, or walnuts to this guilt-free chocolate lovers' recipe.

Coconut oil spray
¼ cup coconut oil, butter, or ghee
1 cup coconut sugar or organic
    cane sugar
1 cup unsweetened cocoa powder
2 teaspoons pure vanilla extract
4 large organic, cage-free eggs
Pinch of sea salt

Preheat the oven to 350°F and spray a 9-inch square baking dish with coconut oil spray.

Melt the coconut oil in a saucepan over low heat, then stir in sugar, cocoa powder, and vanilla until well combined. Whisk in the eggs and the sea salt until the batter is well combined, then pour into the prepared baking dish. Bake for 25 to 30 minutes, until a toothpick inserted into the center comes out clean. Remove from the oven and let cool before slicing into bars.

Healthy Crispy Rice Bars

Makes 13 to 15 (1-inch) bars

A fun little twist on an old-school classic, but upgraded with all real-food ingredients!

2 tablespoons coconut oil

½ cup pure maple syrup

½ cup honey

½ cup almond butter, or other nut butter of your choice

2 teaspoons pure vanilla extract

5½ cups gluten-free puffed brown rice or millet cereal

½ cup dark chocolate chips (optional)

Line a 9-by-11-inch baking dish with parchment paper.

Combine the coconut oil, maple syrup, honey, almond butter, and vanilla in a small saucepan over low heat and stir until well mixed. Remove from the heat.

Place the cereal and chocolate chips, if using, in a medium bowl and drizzle warm mixture over the cereal. Gently stir to combine. Pour the cereal mixture into the prepared dish and press it flat with a rubber spatula or back of a large spoon. Chill in the fridge for at least 1 hour before cutting and serving. Store in the fridge until ready to eat.

Chocolate Chip Olive Oil Cookies

Makes 12 medium or 24 mini cookies

This is my favorite version of a chocolate chip cookie. The olive oil adds a layer of richness and gooeyness that's hard to beat, and even the biggest cookie connoisseurs won't know this is gluten-free!

1 cup almond meal

¼ cup coconut flour (or more almond meal, though you'll get a slightly softer texture)

½ cup coconut sugar

¼ cup olive oil

1 large organic, cage-free egg

¼ cup chocolate chips

2 tablespoons cocoa nibs

1 teaspoon pure vanilla extract

½ teaspoon baking soda

Pinch of sea salt, plus more for sprinkling

Preheat the oven to 350°F and line a baking sheet with parchment paper.

Mix all the ingredients together in a medium bowl and scoop into 12 to 14 rounded cookies depending on your size preference, spacing them about one inch apart. Bake for 7 to 9 minutes for mini cookies, or 10 to 12 minutes for medium ones. Sprinkle with sea salt when done.

Flourless Chocolate Crinkle Cookies

Makes 24 cookies

All the chocolate and all the cookie goodness, but without the flour. If you try to remove these cookies from the pan when they are warm, they'll stick and break. So, patience, my darling. It's worth it. For a variation with a bittersweet crunch, I like using ¼ cup of chocolate chips and ¼ cup of cocoa nibs.

4 large organic, cage-free egg whites

3 cups powdered sugar

¾ cup unsweetened cocoa powder

1 tablespoon pure vanilla extract

Pinch of sea salt

½ cup dark mini chocolate chips or finely chopped dark chocolate

Preheat the oven to 350°F and line two baking sheets with parchment paper.

Whisk the egg whites in a medium bowl, using an electric mixer. Mix together the powdered sugar and cocoa powder in a separate large bowl. Add the vanilla, sea salt, and whipped egg whites to the cocoa mixture. Stir well to combine. Then, add the chocolate chips and continue to stir.

Scoop 24 teaspoon-size balls of batter and space evenly on the prepared baking sheet. Bake for 10 minutes, or until they begin to crinkle and crack slightly. Remove and let cool completely before carefully removing from the baking sheet with a spatula.

Ice-Cream Sandwiches

Makes 4 servings

The most fun summer dessert has been upgraded! I love these for a cheeky make-ahead dessert that turns everyone around the table into their childhood selves. Start with a thin gluten-free cookie of your choice: Chocolate Chip Olive Oil Cookies (page 235), Flourless Chocolate Crinkle Cookies (page 236), or a store-bought version. Fun flavor combinations can include vanilla ice cream + gingersnaps, chocolate ice cream + chocolate chip cookies, mango sorbet + coconut cookies, and so on. Keeps well in the freezer for up to one month.

1 pint organic gelato, ice cream, coconut milk ice cream, or sorbet of your choice
8 gluten-free cookies
Sprinkle of sea salt (optional)

Let the ice cream container warm on the counter for 1 to 2 minutes while you get your cookies ready to assemble. Tear four small sheets of plastic wrap and place on the counter, and place a cookie in the middle of each. Place a scoop of ice cream on the cookie and mash down slightly with your fingers before adding a second cookie on top. Sprinkle with sea salt, if using. Wrap in the plastic wrap and place in the freezer.

Repeat for the rest of the cookies. Freeze for at least 1 hour before serving.

SIPS

Healthy Cocktails to Cin-Cin and Cheers

The Pink Cadillac   244

Cucumber Mint Margarita   244

The Palm Springs   247

The Spicy Cabo   248

Spicy Cilantro Mule   248

The Garden Goddess   251

The Aviator   251

Mezcal Negroni   252

The Lime in the Coconut   255

Maple Old-Fashioned   256

Butterscotch Old-Fashioned   256

The Kombucha Spritz   259

Blueberry Shrub   260

Celery, Cucumber, and Lime Tonic Mocktail   263

Maple Lemonade   264

Cocktails can have a bad rap, and for good reason.
Traditional ones are often full of extra sugar, chemical
sweeteners, hidden dyes, and low-quality alcohol. But
with a few swaps and more attention to the quality of
ingredients, healthier cocktails are not only possible,
but can be such a beautiful addition to a healthy life,
when savored and enjoyed with intention.

HOW TO STOCK YOUR BAR FOR HEALTHIER COCKTAILS

Club soda base: a great tool to use to add extra volume and texture without any added sweetener

High-quality alcohol: organic, local, or small-batch vodka, gin, tequila, or whiskey

Citrus/bitters/vinegars: orange, lemon, lime, grapefruit, bitters, digestifs (Campari, Bénedictine, falernum, Fernet) or cider vinegar

Natural sweeteners: Cointreau, natural tonic water, kombucha, shrub, green Chartreuse, homemade honey simple syrup, pure maple syrup

Garnishes: herbs, citrus peels, vegetables, pickled vegetables

Ice: in most cases

Supplies: Having a variety of fun cocktail glasses (vintage coupes, short tumblers, champagne flutes), large ice cubes, a great shaker, garnish materials, and a good paring knife makes the cocktail-making experience more personal and intentional, and can allow you to really savor the process, and to help make cocktail making more of an art and beautiful ritual instead of just a drink.

HOW TO MAKE INFUSIONS AT HOME

Creating your own natural cocktail infusions at home can quickly elevate your home cocktail experience. It's truly the best and healthiest way to add tons of flavor without extra sugar. Infusions can be done with the base spirit itself (a jalapeño- or ginger-infused tequila, let's say) or with a homemade syrup (thyme-lavender honey, anyone?).

To make syrup: Combine 1 cup of water and ¼ cup of pure maple syrup, honey, or black-strap molasses, plus any of the following flavor elements, in a saucepan. Bring to a boil then let simmer for 10 to 15 minutes. For a stronger flavor, place the mixture in a mason jar or glass storage container with a lid, and store in the fridge for 24 to 48 hours before straining as needed. Store in the fridge for up to three months.

To make a spirit-based infusion: Add any of the following to the spirit of your choice, in a large glass mason jar or glass storage container with a lid. Let the mixture sit at room temperature for a minimum of 24 hours, and up to 72 hours, to infuse before removing the flavor element and storing the remaining liquid in a sealed container.

Natural Flavor Elements:

Apples

Berries

Chiles

Cinnamon sticks

Cucumber, sliced

Ginger, freshly peeled

Grapefruit

Herbs

Jalapeño peppers

Lemon

Lime

Orange

Tea, brewed

The Pink Cadillac

Makes 2 servings

Fact: Campari is definitely a bar essential to keep around. It's an Italian bitters that aids with digestion, and fact: its fun pink color alone will make you happy.

3 ounces tequila

1½ ounces Campari

3 ounces St-Germain

Juice of 1 orange

Ice

Twists of orange for garnish

Combine all the ingredients, except the orange twists, in a cocktail shaker. Shake until cold and strain into two coupe or cocktail glasses. Garnish with a twist of orange.

Cucumber Mint Margarita

Makes 4 servings

A fun fresh twist on my favorite signature margarita recipe.

4 ounces tequila

3 ounces Cointreau

Juice of 4 limes

¼ cucumber, peeled and sliced

Leaves from 4 mint sprigs,
    plus more for garnish

Ice

Club soda

1 lime, cut into wedges

Combine the tequila, Cointreau, lime juice, cucumber, mint, and ice in a cocktail shaker. Shake until cold. Fill four cocktail glasses one-quarter full with club soda and ice and strain the margarita mixture on top. Stir gently and garnish with lime wedges and fresh mint leaves.

The Pink Cadillac

The Palm Springs

Makes 2 servings

Inspired by the retro vibes of this desert town, this cocktail is made to be sipped as close to a pool as possible.

Juice of 1 grapefruit

Juice of 1 lime

3 ounces vodka or gin

2 ounces Cointreau

Ice

Club soda (optional)

Jalapeño slices and/or hibiscus
flowers, for garnish

Combine all the ingredients, except the club soda and citrus garnishes, in a cocktail shaker. Shake and strain over two pretty cocktail glasses filled with ice. Add club soda for a dash of fizz, if you wish. Garnish the drinks with an extra lime wedge or grapefruit peel.

The Spicy Cabo

Makes 2 servings

A little taste of the Mexican Mediterranean, no matter where you live. Garnish with an extra jalapeño, or lime or lemon peel.

Juice of ½ lemon
Juice of 1 lime
6 thin slices jalapeño pepper
3 ounces vodka, tequila, or mezcal
2 ounces Cointreau
Ice
Club soda (optional)

Combine all the ingredients, except the club soda, in a shaker. Shake and strain into two cocktail glasses filled with ice. Add club soda, if you like.

Spicy Cilantro Mule

Makes 2 servings

Traditional mules are made with ginger beer, which you can always swap in for the club soda if you prefer sweeter drinks, but I love this less sweet version.

3 ounces vodka
1½ ounces Cointreau
Juice of 1 lime
Handful of fresh cilantro leaves
2 slices jalapeño pepper
One ½-inch piece fresh ginger, grated
Ice
6 ounces club soda

Combine all the ingredients, except the club soda, in a cocktail shaker. Fill two glasses halfway with ice, split the club soda between the glasses, and strain the cocktail mixture between the two glasses.

The Spicy Cabo

The Garden Goddess

The Garden Goddess

Makes 4 servings

Garden fresh and one of the most refreshing cocktails. If you don't have Lillet, swap it out for a splash of natural tonic water, or a honey simple syrup. Tip: If you want to add a lemon twist garnish to your drinks, make sure you peel the lemon first, then juice the insides according to the recipe.

6 ounces vodka or gin

4 ounces Lillet

Juice of 1 lemon

Ice

6 dill fronds, removed from the stem, plus more for garnish

8 basil leaves, plus more for garnish

4 large cocktail ice cubes for serving

Lemon twists for garnish (optional)

Combine the vodka or gin, Lillet, and lemon juice in a cocktail shaker with ice. Shake well and strain into four coupe or cocktail glasses. Garnish each glass with a large cocktail ice cube, a basil leaf, a dill frond, and lemon twist, if using.

The Aviator

Makes 2 servings

For building out a healthy bar, Bénédictine and green Chartreuse are my two favorite liqueurs, because their flavors are just slightly sweet, but not overly so. Bénédictine has a bit of a spicy flavor, whereas green Chartreuse is more herbal. Using them together or separately enables you to skip the added sugar, while getting a beautifully made cocktail. This one is my current favorite when we do date nights in and I want something that feels a little bespoke and fancy.

1½ ounces Bénédictine

3 ounces gin

1½ ounces green Chartreuse

Juice of 2 limes

Ice

2 strips lime peel

Combine all the ingredients, except the lime peel, in a cocktail shaker. Shake until cold and strain into two martini glasses to serve. Garnish each with a lime peel.

Mezcal Negroni

Makes 2 servings

A smoky twist on a regular Negroni, which is a classic Italian drink made with the bitter aperitif Campari. Bitters are a great digestif to have before or with meals and can actually help with digestion.

2 ounces Campari

2 ounces mezcal

2 ounces sweet vermouth

Ice

2 large cocktail ice cubes for
    serving

2 strips orange peel for garnish

Combine all the ingredients, except the large ice cubes and orange peel, in a cocktail shaker. Place a large ice cube in each of two cocktail glasses. Shake the mixture until cold, then strain between the two glasses. Garnish each with an orange twist.

The Lime in the Coconut

Makes 2 servings

Just like it sounds: a tropical vacation in a glass, but minus the loads of sugar and chemicals! For this drink, I have the best luck using the thicker part of coconut milk from the can, shaken together with the other ingredients or blended beforehand until it's smooth.

6 ounces vodka

6 basil leaves

Juice of 2 limes

6 tablespoons coconut milk

Ice

Cointreau (optional)

Lime wedges for garnish

Combine all the ingredients, except the Cointreau and lime wedges, in a cocktail shaker. Shake well and strain into two coupe or cocktail glasses with ice. Add a splash of Cointreau to sweeten, if needed. Garnish with a lime wedge.

Maple Old-Fashioned

Makes 2 servings

This is a recipe from our wedding, and always our go-to house cocktail when people come over.

3 ounces bourbon

2 teaspoons pure maple syrup

4 dashes bitters

Ice

2 large cocktail ice cubes

2 strips orange peel for garnish

Combine all the ingredients, except the large ice cubes and orange peels, in a cocktail shaker. Stir quickly with a spoon to chill and combine the liquids. Place 1 large ice cube in each of two cocktail glasses, and strain cocktail between the two glasses. Garnish each with an orange peel.

Butterscotch Old-Fashioned

Makes 2 servings

I've never been much of a whiskey girl, until I created this little concoction a few winters ago. Inspired by my mom's love around the holidays of a postdinner sip of Frangelico, which is a sweet after-dinner drink for sipping. It's a little too sweet for me on its own but in place of a sweetener? It's pretty perfect.

3 ounces whiskey

2 dashes orange bitters

Juice of ¼ sweet orange

1½ ounces Frangelico

Ice

2 large cocktail ice cubes

2 strips orange peel for garnish

Combine all the ingredients, except the large ice cubes and orange peel, in a cocktail shaker. Shake and strain, into two of your favorite cocktail glasses, garnishing each with a large ice cube and an orange peel.

Maple Old-Fashioned

The Kombucha Spritz

Makes 2 servings

A cocktail with helpful digestive and immune system-boosting properties? Yes, please. Other fun additions to this drink could be a splash of shrub, a dash of Cointreau to sweeten just a touch, or using any flavor of kombucha you prefer.

2 cups ginger kombucha

3 ounces vodka or gin

1 cup ice

2 sage leaves, rosemary sprigs, slices of lemon, or candied ginger to garnish

Split the kombucha between two wineglasses, and add the vodka or gin. Stir well before adding ice and the garnishes of your choice.

Blueberry Shrub

Makes 4 servings

A shrub is a homemade vinegar soda that pairs perfectly with club soda, or mixed into cocktails instead of a sweetener. I love it mocktail style on nights I don't want to drink but want to have something more special than water. The cider vinegar is a great digestive aid, too! Raspberries, cherries, strawberries, peaches, and plums would all work well in this recipe. It's a perfect way to use fruit that's about to turn.

1 cup cider vinegar
2 cups blueberries
1 cup unrefined cane sugar
   or coconut sugar

Combine the vinegar and fruit in a glass mason jar with a lid and refrigerate for at least two days, and up to three months.

When ready to serve, strain the fruit out of the vinegar mixture and discard. Place all the liquid in a saucepan with the sugar and bring to a boil. Boil for 3 minutes. Let cool before pouring into a glass mason jar to store in the fridge for up to eight weeks.

For mocktails, add ¼ cup of the shrub to ice and water, sparkling water, or kombucha. For cocktails, use in place of a sweetener or mixer. Garnish with extra fruit wedges or skewers, to serve.

Celery, Cucumber, and Lime Tonic Mocktail

Makes 2 servings

A juicer is recommended but not necessary for this one. Natural tonic waters will be made with real sugar instead of high-fructose corn syrup and are an amazing staple to keep around. Optional to add gin or vodka, of course.

3 celery stalks

1 cucumber

2 limes

1 cup club soda

1 cup natural tonic water

Ice

Juice the celery, cucumber, and lime with a juicer, or blend together in a blender and strain out the pulp.

Split the club soda and tonic evenly between two glasses, pour the celery mixture on top, and add ice to serve.

Maple Lemonade

Makes 4 servings

Feel free to adjust the amount of maple syrup to your liking. Sliced lemons and fresh mint make beautiful garnishes, as does freezing this mixture in ice pop molds.

¼ cup pure maple syrup

Juice of 4 lemons, strained of seeds

Ice

Heat 1 cup of the water in a medium saucepan until warm and stir in the maple syrup until it dissolves. Add the lemon juice and 7 additional cups of water and chill in the fridge until you're ready to serve over ice.

CONVERSIONS

THE STANDARD GRADATED SYSTEM OF US MEASURES

1 teaspoon	1 cup
1 tablespoon = 3 teaspoons	1 pint = 2 cups
1/4 cup = 4 tablespoons	1 quart = 4 cups
1/2 cup = 8 tablespoons	1 gallon = 4 quarts

VOLUME

US Standard	UK Imperial	Fluid Ounces	Practical Metric Equivalent
1 teaspoon	1 teaspoon		5 ml
2 teaspoons	2 teaspoons	1/4 fl oz	10 ml
1 tablespoon	1 tablespoon	1/2 fl oz	15 ml
1 1/2 tablespoons	1 1/2 tablespoons	3/4 fl oz	22.5 ml
2 tablespoons	2 tablespoons	1 fl oz	30 ml
3 tablespoons	3 tablespoons	1 1/2 fl oz	45 ml
1/4 cup (4 tablespoons)	4 tablespoons	2 fl oz	60 ml
1/3 cup		2 1/2 fl oz	75 ml
1/2 cup		4 fl oz	125 ml
2/3 cup	1/4 pint or 1 gill	5 fl oz	150 ml
3/4 cup		6 fl oz	185 ml
1 cup		8 fl oz	250 ml
1 1/4 cups	1/2 pint	10 fl oz	300 ml
1 1/2 cups		12 fl oz	375 ml
2 cups		16 fl oz	500 ml
2 1/2 cups	1 pint	20 fl oz	600 ml
1 quart (4 cups)	1 2/3 pints	32 fl oz	1 liter
2 quarts (8 cups)		64 fl oz	2 liters
1 gallon (4 qts)		128 fl oz	4 liters

Exact conversion: 1 fluid ounce = 29.57 milliliters

WEIGHT

US Standard in Ounces	US Standard in Pounds	Practical Metric Equivalent
½ oz		15 g
1 oz		25 g
2 oz		50 g
4 oz	¼ lb	125 g
5¼ oz	⅓ lb	150 g
8 oz	½ lb	225 g
12 oz	¾ lb	350 g
16 oz	1 lb	450–500 g
24 oz	1½ lb	750 g
32 oz	2 lb	1 kg

Exact conversion: 1 ounce = 28.35 grams

LENGTH

Imperial	Metric
¼ inch	0.5 cm
½ inch	1 cm
1 inch	2.5 cm
6 inches	15 cm
1 foot (12 inches)	30 cm

Exact conversion: 1 inch = 2.54 cm

OVEN TEMPERATURES

Fahrenheit	Celsius	Gas Mark	Description
250	120	½	very low
275	140	1	very low
300	150	2	low
325	160	3	low/moderate
350	175	4	moderate
375	190	5	moderately hot
400	200	6	hot
425	220	7	very hot
450	230	8	very hot

INDEX

A

ahi tuna: Seared Ahi and Crab Ceviche, 119
almond butter
    Carrot Noodle Pad Thai, 173
    Healthy Crispy Rice Bars, 232
    Matcha Vanilla Energy Balls, 138
    Snickerdoodle Energy Balls, 138
    Superfood Butter and Banana Bites, 143
almond flour: Winter Greens Gratin, 196
almond meal
    Blackberry Scones, 86
    Chocolate Chip Olive Oil Cookies, 235
    Healthy Maple Graham Crackers, 228
    Honey Butter and Oatmeal Breakfast Cookies, 59
    Kale Feta Bread, 94
    Mini Pumpkin Spice Doughnuts (or Muffins), 75
    Seasonal Jam Dots, 62
    Sweet Potato Morning Muffins, 70
almond milk
    The Busy Girl Smoothie, 52
    Homemade Corn Muffins, 93
    Life-Changing Gluten-Free Waffles, 89
    Snickerdoodle Energy Balls, 138
almonds
    Cinnamon Chocolate Energy Balls, 142
    Homemade Nut Milk, 42
anchovies
    Baja Chopped Caesar Salad, 116
    Grilled Shrimp and Kale Caesar Salad, 174
    The Warm Shaved Brussels Sprout Caesar, 171
    Whipped Feta Dip, 152
The Anytime Breakfast Bowl, 61
apples
    Apple Pie Bars, 83
    The Everyday Chicken Salad, 109
    The Fall Salad You Won't Be Able to Quit, 124
apricots, dried
    Kale and Quinoa Salad with Squash, Apricots, and Bacon, 127
    Vanilla Apricot Granola Bars, 144
arugula
    Quinoa, Feta, Dill, and Garbanzo Bean Salad, 112
    Sweet Potato Waffles with Fried Eggs, 80
    Tomato Salad with Feta and Pistachios, 218
The Aviator, 251
avocados
    Baja Chopped Caesar Salad, 116
    The Cobb Job Salad, 110
    Everyday Smoothie Bowls, 46
    The Fall Salad You Won't Be Able to Quit, 124
    Grilled Broccoli and Avocado with Sesame Seeds, 216
    Homemade Avocado Mayo, 109
    Huevos Rancheros Bake, 90

    The Lemon Feta Salad, 115
    Salmon Niçoise Salad with Sarah's Daily Basil Dressing, 102
    The Sister A.G.T.O. Salad, 123
    Spicy Chicken Burgers or Meatballs, 188
    Summer Picnic Poblano Salad, 105

B

Baja Chopped Caesar Salad, 116
baked beans: Sweet Potato Turkey Chili, 200
bananas
    The Busy Girl Smoothie, 52
    Butternut Squash and Cardamom Pancakes, 84
    Carrot, Turmeric, and Ginger Smoothie, 50
    Chocolate Green Smoothies, 49
    Everyday Smoothie Bowls, 46
    Superfood Butter and Banana Bites, 143
    Zucchini Bread, 87
basil
    Broccoli, Basil, and Goat Cheese Pizzas, 184
    Carrot Noodle Pad Thai, 173
    Daily Basil Dressing, 102
    The Fall Salad You Won't Be Able to Quit, 124
    The Garden Goddess, 251
    Gigante Bean and Tomato Bake, 194
    Green Bean, Cantaloupe, and Basil Salad, 214
    Herby Green Rice, 187
    Homemade Summer Pesto, 106
    The Lime in the Coconut, 255
    Thai Crab Cucumber Salad, 128
beets
    The Cutie Pink Hummus, 155
    Red Raspberry and Beet Smoothie Bowl, 46
bell peppers
    Bloody Mary Shrimp Cocktails, 160
    Cauliflower Rice Cups, 58
    Coconut Green Curry Snapper Bowls, 179
    Crustless Chicken Sausage and Veggie Pizza, 167
    The Real Greek Salad, 100
    Spicy Tomato Shakshuka, 76
    Summer Picnic Poblano Salad, 105
    Sweet Potato Turkey Chili, 200
    Turkey Sausage and Veggie Polenta Bowls, 190
    Veggie Bowls with Coconut Lime Parsley Sauce, 202
Blackberry Scones, 86
Bloody Mary Shrimp Cocktails, 160
Blueberry Shrub, 260
bok choy: Veggie Bowls with Coconut Lime Parsley Sauce, 202
broccoli
    Broccoli, Basil, and Goat Cheese Pizzas, 184

    Broccoli Rice Paella, 180
    Cauliflower Rice Cups, 58
    Grilled Broccoli and Avocado with Sesame Seeds, 216
    The Italian Situation, 199
    The Morning Warming Smoothie, 53
    Smoked Salmon Pasta with Cashew Alfredo Sauce, 183
brown rice pasta: Smoked Salmon Pasta with Cashew Alfredo Sauce, 183
brown rice pizza crust: Broccoli, Basil, and Goat Cheese Pizzas, 184
Brussels sprouts
    Roasted Sheet Pan Chicken and Veggies, 176
    The Warm Shaved Brussels Sprout Caesar, 171
buckwheat groats: Veggie Bowls with Coconut Lime Parsley Sauce, 202
The Busy Girl Smoothie, 52
butter lettuce
    The Fall Salad You Won't Be Able to Quit, 124
    Salmon Niçoise Salad with Sarah's Daily Basil Dressing, 102
Butternut Squash and Cardamom Pancakes, 84
Butternut Squash and Sage Risotto, 193
Butterscotch Old-Fashioned, 256

C

cantaloupe: Green Bean, Cantaloupe, and Basil Salad, 214
carrots
    The Anytime Breakfast Bowl, 61
    Carrot, Turmeric, and Ginger Smoothie, 50
    Carrot Noodle Pad Thai, 173
    Coconut Green Curry Snapper Bowls, 179
    Cozy Sausage and Lentil Stew, 169
    Crustless Chicken Sausage and Veggie Pizza, 167
    Healthy Veggie Noodle Pho, 132
    The Italian Situation, 199
    Roasted Cauliflower, Carrot, and Tahini Salad, 120
    Roasted Sheet Pan Chicken and Veggies, 176
    Sweet Potato Turkey Chili, 200
    Turkey Sausage and Veggie Polenta Bowls, 190
    Veggie Bowls with Coconut Lime Parsley Sauce, 202
cashews
    Smoked Salmon Pasta with Cashew Alfredo Sauce, 183
    Vanilla Apricot Granola Bars, 144
cauliflower
    Cauliflower Rice Cups, 58
    Coconut Green Curry Snapper Bowls, 179
    Roasted Cauliflower, Carrot, and Tahini Salad, 120

celery
Bloody Mary Shrimp Cocktails, 160
Celery, Cucumber, and Lime Tonic Mocktail, 263
Cozy Sausage and Lentil Stew, 169
The Everyday Chicken Salad, 109
Sweet Potato Turkey Chili, 200
chia seeds
Coconut, Coffee, and Cocoa Nib Overnight "Oats," 56
Golden Milk Pots of Gold, 55
Grain-Free Seedy Bread, 69
Honey Butter and Oatmeal Breakfast Cookies, 59
chicken
Broccoli, Basil, and Goat Cheese Pizzas, 184
Broccoli Rice Paella, 180
The Cobb Job Salad, 110
Crispy Italian Chicken Wings, 159
The Everyday Chicken Salad, 109
Pesto, Quinoa, and Tomato Salad, 106
Poblano Chicken Tortilla Soup, 205
The Real Greek Salad, 100
Roasted Sheet Pan Chicken and Veggies, 176
The Sister A.G.T.O. Salad, 123
Spicy Chicken Burgers or Meatballs, 188
Summer Picnic Poblano Salad, 105
chicken sausage: Crustless Chicken Sausage and Veggie Pizza, 167
chickpeas. *See* garbanzo beans
chili powder: Sweet Potato Turkey Chili, 200
Chilled Cucumber Gazpacho, 163
chipotle chiles
Herby Roasted Corn Salad, 213
Spicy Chicken Burgers or Meatballs, 188
chocolate
Chocolate Chip Olive Oil Cookies, 235
Cookie Dough Energy Balls, 138
Flourless Chocolate Crinkle Cookies, 236
Flourless Everything Cookies, 224
Mint Chocolate Coconut Milkshakes, 227
Salted Dark Chocolate Peanut Butter Cups, 226
cinnamon
Apple Pie Bars, 83
Butternut Squash and Cardamom Pancakes, 84
Cinnamon Chocolate Energy Balls, 142
Coconut, Coffee, and Cocoa Nib Overnight "Oats," 56
Cranberry Walnut Grain-Free Granola, 65
Earl Grey Cinnamon Latte, 40
Healing Golden Milk Paste, 39
Healthy Maple Graham Crackers, 228
Maca Hot Chocolate, 36
Mini Pumpkin Spice Doughnuts (or Muffins), 75
The Morning Warming Smoothie, 53
Snickerdoodle Energy Balls, 138
Sweet Potato Morning Muffins, 70
Zucchini Bread, 87
The Cobb Job Salad, 110

cocktails
The Aviator, 251
Butterscotch Old-Fashioned, 256
Cucumber Mint Margarita, 244
The Garden Goddess, 251
The Kombucha Spritz, 259
The Lime in the Coconut, 255
Maple Old-Fashioned, 256
Mezcal Negroni, 252
The Palm Springs, 247
The Pink Cadillac, 244
The Spicy Cabo, 248
Spicy Cilantro Mule, 248
cocoa nibs
Chocolate Chip Olive Oil Cookies, 235
Chocolate Green Smoothies, 49
Coconut and Cocoa Nib Balls, 141
Coconut, Coffee, and Cocoa Nib Overnight "Oats," 56
Matcha Vanilla Energy Balls, 138
Spirulina Energy Balls, 138
Superfood Butter and Banana Bites, 143
cocoa powder
Cinnamon Chocolate Energy Balls, 142
Coconut and Cocoa Nib Balls, 141
Date Hot Chocolate, 36
Flourless Brownies, 231
Flourless Chocolate Crinkle Cookies, 236
Maca Hot Chocolate, 36
Coconut Curry Sauce, 179
coconut, flakes or shredded
Blackberry Scones, 86
Cinnamon Chocolate Energy Balls, 142
Coconut and Cocoa Nib Balls, 141
Coconut, Coffee, and Cocoa Nib Overnight "Oats," 56
Flourless Everything Cookies, 224
Supereasy Energy Balls, 138
Superfood Butter and Banana Bites, 143
Vanilla Apricot Granola Bars, 144
Coconut Green Curry Snapper Bowls, 179
coconut milk, canned or carton
Coconut Green Curry Snapper Bowls, 179
Golden Milk Pots of Gold, 55
The Lime in the Coconut, 255
Mint Chocolate Coconut Milk Shakes, 227
Roasted Kabocha Squash Soup, 135
Veggie Bowls with Coconut Lime Parsley Sauce, 202
coffee, brewed
Coconut, Coffee, and Cocoa Nib Overnight "Oats," 56
Coffee Chocolate Green Buzz Smoothie, 49
Healthy Pumpkin Spice Latte, 35
coffee beans: Vanilla Cold Brew, 32
conversions, 266
Cookie Dough Energy Balls, 138
corn
Herby Roasted Corn Salad, 213
Summer Picnic Poblano Salad, 105
cornmeal: Homemade Corn Muffins, 93
Cozy Roasted Parsnip Soup, 129
Cozy Sausage and Lentil Stew, 169
crab
Seared Ahi and Crab Ceviche, 119

Thai Crab Cucumber Salad, 128
cranberries
Cranberry Walnut Grain-Free Granola, 65
Vanilla Apricot Granola Bars, 144
Crispy Brown Butter Sole with Herby Green Rice, 187
Crispy Italian Chicken Wings, 159
Crustless Chicken Sausage and Veggie Pizza, 167
cucumber
Bloody Mary Shrimp Cocktails, 160
Celery, Cucumber, and Lime Tonic Mocktail, 263
Chilled Cucumber Gazpacho, 163
Cucumber Mint Margarita, 244
The Real Greek Salad, 100
Seared Ahi and Crab Ceviche, 119
Thai Crab Cucumber Salad, 128
The Cutie Pink Hummus, 155

D
daikon radishes: Thai Crab Cucumber Salad, 128
Daily Basil Dressing, 103
dark chocolate
Healthy Crispy Rice Bars, 232
Mint Chocolate Coconut Milk Shakes, 227
Salted Dark Chocolate Peanut Butter Cups, 226
dates
Cinnamon Chocolate Energy Balls, 142
Date Hot Chocolate, 36
Mint Chocolate Green Smoothie, 49

E
Earl Grey Cinnamon Latte, 40
eggplant: Savory Yogurt Bowls, 66
eggs
The Anytime Breakfast Bowl, 61
Cauliflower Rice Cups, 58
The Cobb Job Salad, 110
Huevos Rancheros Bake, 90
Salmon Niçoise Salad with Sarah's Daily Basil Dressing, 102
Spicy Tomato Shakshuka, 76
Sweet Potato Waffles with Fried Eggs, 80
The Everyday Chicken Salad, 109
Everyday Smoothie Bowls, 46

F
The Fall Salad You Won't Be Able to Quit, 124
feta
Kale Feta Bread, 94
The Lemon Feta Salad, 115
Quinoa, Feta, Dill, and Garbanzo Bean Salad, 112
The Real Greek Salad, 100
Tomato Salad with Feta and Pistachios, 218
Whipped Feta Dip, 152
Flourless Brownies, 231
Flourless Chocolate Crinkle Cookies, 236
Flourless Everything Cookies, 224

G

garbanzo bean flour: Socca Flatbread, 151
garbanzo beans
    The Cutie Pink Hummus, 155
    Garbanzo Bean Crunchies, 158
    Quinoa, Feta, Dill, and Garbanzo Bean
      Salad, 112
The Garden Goddess, 251
garlic
    Chilled Cucumber Gazpacho, 163
    Cozy Sausage and Lentil Stew, 169
    The Cutie Pink Hummus, 155
    Poblano Chicken Tortilla Soup, 205
    Spicy Tomato Shakshuka, 76
ghee: Healing Golden Milk Paste, 39
Gigante Bean and Tomato Bake, 194
ginger
    Carrot Noodle Pad Thai, 173
    Carrot, Turmeric, and Ginger
      Smoothie, 50
    Veggie Bowls with Coconut Lime Pars-
      ley Sauce, 203
    Healing Golden Milk Paste, 39
    Healthy Veggie Noodle Pho, 132
    The Kombucha Spritz, 259
    Spicy Cilantro Mule, 248
goat cheese
    Broccoli, Basil, and Goat Cheese
      Pizzas, 184
    The Sister A.G.T.O. Salad, 123
Golden Milk Pots of Gold, 55
Golden Milk Turmeric Latte, 39
Grain-Free Seedy Bread, 69
grapefruit juice: The Palm Springs, 247
grapes
    Chilled Cucumber Gazpacho, 163
    The Everyday Chicken Salad, 109
green beans
    Green Bean, Cantaloupe, and Basil
      Salad, 214
    The Green Bean Dream, 209
    Salmon Niçoise Salad with Sarah's
      Daily Basil Dressing, 102
Green Kale Smoothie Bowl, 46
green onions
    Broccoli, Basil, and Goat Cheese
      Pizzas, 184
    Cauliflower Rice Cups, 58
    Herby Green Rice, 187
    Herby Roasted Corn Salad, 213
    Seared Ahi and Crab Ceviche, 119
    Skillet Potato Pancake with Green
      Onions and Chives, 79
Grilled Broccoli and Avocado with Ses-
    ame Seeds, 216
Grilled Shrimp and Kale Caesar Salad, 174
ground turkey
    Cozy Sausage and Lentil Stew, 169
    Sweet Potato Turkey Chili, 200
    Turkey Sausage and Veggie Polenta
      Bowls, 190

H

Healing Golden Milk Paste, 39
Healthy Crispy Rice Bars, 232
Healthy Maple Graham Crackers, 228
Healthy Pumpkin Spice Latte, 35
Healthy Veggie Noodle Pho, 132

Herby Green Rice, 187
Herby Parmesan Polenta, 190
Herby Roasted Corn Salad, 213
Homemade Avocado Mayo, 109
Homemade Corn Muffins, 93
Homemade Nut Milk, 42
Homemade Summer Pesto, 106
honey
    Carrot Noodle Pad Thai, 173
    Coconut Green Curry Snapper Bowls,
      179
    Golden Milk Turmeric Latte, 39
    Healthy Crispy Rice Bars, 232
    Honey Butter and Oatmeal Breakfast
      Cookies, 59
    Rosemary and Sea Salt Crackers, 156
    Vanilla Apricot Granola Bars, 144
Huevos Rancheros Bake, 90
The Husband Fries, 210

I

Ice-Cream Sandwiches, 239
infusions, for cocktails, 243
The Italian Situation, 199

J

jalapeño peppers
    Healthy Veggie Noodle Pho, 132
    The Palm Springs, 247
    The Spicy Cabo, 248
    Spicy Cilantro Mule, 248
jicama
    Bloody Mary Shrimp Cocktails, 160
    Seared Ahi and Crab Ceviche, 119

K

Kalamata olives: The Sister A.G.T.O.
    Salad, 123
kale
    The Anytime Breakfast Bowl, 61
    The Busy Girl Smoothie, 52
    Green Kale Smoothie Bowl, 46
    Grilled Shrimp and Kale Caesar Salad,
      174
    Kale and Quinoa Salad with Squash,
      Apricots, and Bacon, 127
    Kale Feta Bread, 94
    Spicy Tomato Shakshuka, 76
    Turkey Sausage and Veggie Polenta
      Bowls, 190
    Winter Greens Gratin, 196
The Kombucha Spritz, 259

L

lemon juice
    Apple Pie Bars, 83
    Broccoli, Basil, and Goat Cheese
      Pizzas, 184
    Crispy Italian Chicken Wings, 159
    The Cutie Pink Hummus, 155
    The Everyday Chicken Salad, 109
    The Garden Goddess, 251
    Grilled Shrimp and Kale Caesar Salad,
      174
    Homemade Avocado Mayo, 109
    Homemade Summer Pesto, 106
    The Lemon Feta Salad, 115
    Maple Lemonade, 264
    1-Minute Miracle Sauce, 189

Roasted Cauliflower, Carrot, and
    Tahini Salad, 120
Smoked Salmon Pasta with Cashew
    Alfredo Sauce, 183
The Spicy Cabo, 248
Veggie Bowls with Coconut Lime Pars-
    ley Sauce, 202
The Warm Shaved Brussels Sprout
    Caesar, 171
Whipped Feta Dip, 152
lemons: Savory Yogurt Bowls, 66
lemon zest: The Green Bean Dream, 209
lentils: Cozy Sausage and Lentil Stew, 169
lettuce
    Baja Chopped Caesar Salad, 116
    The Cobb Job Salad, 110
    The Fall Salad You Won't Be Able to
      Quit, 124
    The Lemon Feta Salad, 115
    Quinoa, Feta, Dill, and Garbanzo Bean
      Salad, 112
    Salmon Niçoise Salad with Sarah's
      Daily Basil Dressing, 102
    The Sister A.G.T.O. Salad, 123
    Spicy Chicken Burgers or Meatballs, 188
    Sweet Potato Waffles with Fried Eggs, 80
    Tomato Salad with Feta and Pista-
      chios, 218
Life-Changing Gluten-Free Waffles, 89
lime juice
    The Aviator, 251
    Baja Chopped Caesar Salad, 116
    Bloody Mary Shrimp Cocktails, 160
    Carrot Noodle Pad Thai, 173
    Coconut Green Curry Snapper Bowls,
      179
    Cucumber Mint Margarita, 244
    Herby Roasted Corn Salad, 213
    The Lime in the Coconut, 255
    The Palm Springs, 247
    Seared Ahi and Crab Ceviche, 119
    The Spicy Cabo, 248
    Spicy Cilantro Mule, 248
    Summer Picnic Poblano Salad, 105
    Thai Crab Cucumber Salad, 128
    Veggie Bowls with Coconut Lime Pars-
      ley Sauce, 202
limes
    The Aviator, 251
    Carrot Noodle Pad Thai, 173
    Celery, Cucumber, and Lime Tonic
      Mocktail, 263
    Cucumber Mint Margarita, 244
    The Lime in the Coconut, 255

M

macadamia nut butter: Coconut and
    Cocoa Nib Balls, 141
Maca Hot Chocolate, 36
mango: Carrot, Turmeric, and Ginger
    Smoothie, 50
maple syrup
    Blackberry Scones, 86
    Cinnamon Chocolate Energy Balls, 142
    Coconut and Cocoa Nib Balls, 141
    Coconut, Coffee, and Cocoa Nib Over-
      night "Oats," 56
    Cranberry Walnut Grain-Free Gra-
      nola, 65

Earl Grey Cinnamon Latte, 40
The Fall Salad You Won't Be Able to
    Quit, 124
Healthy Crispy Rice Bars, 232
Healthy Maple Graham Crackers, 228
Healthy Pumpkin Spice Latte, 35
Kale and Quinoa Salad with Squash,
    Apricots, and Bacon, 127
Maple Lemonade, 264
Maple Old-Fashioned, 256
Matcha Vanilla Energy Balls, 138
Seasonal Jam Dots, 62
Snickerdoodles Energy Balls, 138
Sweet Potato Morning Muffins, 70
Thai Crab Cucumber Salad, 128
matcha powder
    Matcha Vanilla Energy Balls, 138
    Sarah's Matcha Latte, 31
Medjool dates: Cinnamon Chocolate
    Energy Balls, 142
Mezcal Negroni, 252
Mini Pumpkin Spice Doughnuts (or
    Muffins), 75
Mint Chocolate Coconut Milkshakes, 227
The Morning Warming Smoothie, 53
mozzarella
    Crustless Chicken Sausage and Veggie
        Pizza, 167
    Gigante Bean and Tomato Bake, 194
    Green Bean, Cantaloupe, and Basil
        Salad, 214

N
nut butters: Green Kale Smoothie Bowl, 46
nut milk
    The Busy Girl Smoothie, 52
    Coconut, Coffee, and Cocoa Nib Over-
        night "Oats," 56
    Coffee Chocolate Green Buzz
        Smoothie, 49
    Date Hot Chocolate, 36
    Golden Milk Turmeric Latte, 39
    Healthy Pumpkin Spice Latte, 35
    Homemade Nut Milk, 42
    Maca Hot Chocolate, 36
    The Morning Warming Smoothie, 53
    Sarah's Matcha Latte, 31
    Sweet Potato Morning Muffins, 70

O
olives
    Salmon Niçoise Salad with Sarah's
        Daily Basil Dressing, 102
    The Sister A.G.T.O. Salad, 123
1-Minute Miracle Sauce, 189
onions
    Bloody Mary Shrimp Cocktails, 160
    Cozy Sausage and Lentil Stew, 169
    The Cutie Pink Hummus, 155
    The Green Bean Dream, 209
    Poblano Chicken Tortilla Soup, 205
    Roasted Kabocha Squash Soup, 135
    Spicy Tomato Shakshuka, 76
    Sweet Potato Turkey Chili, 200
orange juice
    The Pink Cadillac, 244
    Butterscotch Old-Fashioned, 256
oranges
    Butterscotch Old-Fashioned, 256

Carrot, Turmeric, and Ginger
    Smoothie, 50
Maple Old-Fashioned, 256
Mezcal Negroni, 252
The Pink Cadillac, 244

P
The Palm Springs, 247
Parmesan
    Grilled Shrimp and Kale Caesar Salad,
        174
    Herby Parmesan Polenta, 190
    Homemade Summer Pesto, 106
    Winter Greens Gratin, 196
parsnips: Cozy Roasted Parsnip Soup,
    129
peanut butter
    Flourless Everything Cookies, 224
    Salted Dark Chocolate Peanut Butter
        Cups, 226
peas, frozen: Smoked Salmon Pasta with
    Cashew Alfredo Sauce, 183
pesto
    Broccoli, Basil, and Goat Cheese
        Pizzas, 184
    Homemade Summer Pesto, 106
The Pink Cadillac, 244
pistachios: Tomato Salad with Feta and
    Pistachios, 218
poblano peppers
    Poblano Chicken Tortilla Soup, 205
    Spicy Chicken Burgers or Meatballs,
        188
    Summer Picnic Poblano Salad, 105
polenta: Herby Parmesan Polenta, 190
potatoes
    Cozy Roasted Parsnip Soup, 129
    The Husband Fries, 210
    Roasted Sheet Pan Chicken and Veg-
        gies, 176
    Salmon Niçoise Salad with Sarah's
        Daily Basil Dressing, 102
    Skillet Potato Pancake with Green
        Onions and Chives, 79
pumpkin puree
    Healthy Pumpkin Spice Latte, 35
    Mini Pumpkin Spice Doughnuts (or
        Muffins), 75

Q
quinoa
    Kale and Quinoa Salad with Squash,
        Apricots, and Bacon, 127
    Pesto, Quinoa, and Tomato Salad, 106
    Quinoa, Feta, Dill, and Garbanzo Bean
        Salad, 112

R
raspberries: Red Raspberry and Beet
    Smoothie Bowl, 46
The Real Greek Salad, 100
refried pinto beans: Huevos Rancheros
    Bake, 90
rice
    Broccoli Rice Paella, 180
    Butternut Squash and Sage Risotto,
        193
    Herby Green Rice, 187
    The Italian Situation, 199

risotto: Butternut Squash and Sage
    Risotto, 193
Roasted Cauliflower, Carrot, and Tahini
    Salad, 120
Roasted Kabocha Squash Soup, 135
Roasted Sheet Pan Chicken and Veggies,
    176
romaine lettuce: Baja Chopped Caesar
    Salad, 116
rosemary
    Rosemary and Sea Salt Crackers, 156
    Socca Flatbread, 151

S
salads
    Baja Chopped Caesar Salad, 116
    The Cobb Job Salad, 110
    The Fall Salad You Won't Be Able to
        Quit, 124
    Green Bean, Cantaloupe, and Basil
        Salad, 214
    Grilled Shrimp and Kale Caesar Salad,
        174
    Herby Roasted Corn Salad, 213
    Kale and Quinoa Salad with Squash,
        Apricots, and Bacon, 127
    The Lemon Feta Salad, 115
    Pesto, Quinoa, and Tomato Salad,
        106
    Quinoa, Feta, Dill, and Garbanzo Bean
        Salad, 112
    The Real Greek Salad, 100
    Roasted Cauliflower, Carrot, and
        Tahini Salad, 120
    Salmon Niçoise Salad with Sarah's
        Basil Dressing, 102–103
    The Sister A.G.T.O. Salad, 123
    Summer Picnic Poblano Salad, 105
    Thai Crab Cucumber Salad, 128
    Tomato Salad with Feta and Pista-
        chios, 218
    The Warm Shaved Brussels Sprout
        Caesar, 171
salmon
    Baja Chopped Caesar Salad, 116
    Salmon Niçoise Salad with Sarah's
        Daily Basil Dressing, 102–103
    Smoked Salmon Pasta with Cashew
        Alfredo Sauce, 183
Salted Dark Chocolate Peanut Butter
    Cups, 226
Sarah's Matcha Latte, 31
sausage: Winter Greens Gratin, 196
Savory Yogurt Bowls, 66
Seared Ahi and Crab Ceviche, 119
sesame oil: Grilled Broccoli and Avocado
    with Sesame Seeds, 216
sesame seeds
    The Cutie Pink Hummus, 155
    Grain-Free Seedy Bread, 69
    Grilled Broccoli and Avocado with
        Sesame Seeds, 216
Seasonal Jam Dots, 62
shrimp
    Bloody Mary Shrimp Cocktails, 160
    Broccoli Rice Paella, 180
    Grilled Shrimp and Kale Caesar Salad,
        174
The Sister A.G.T.O. Salad, 123

Skillet Potato Pancake with Green Onions and Chives, 79
Smoked Salmon Pasta with Cashew Alfredo Sauce, 183
smoothie bowls: Everyday Smoothie Bowls, 46
smoothies
    The Busy Girl Smoothie, 52
    Carrot, Turmeric, and Ginger Smoothie, 50
    Chocolate Green Smoothies, 49
    The Morning Warming Smoothie, 53
snap peas: The Lemon Feta Salad, 115
Snickerdoodle Energy Balls, 138
snow peas
    Coconut Green Curry Snapper Bowls, 179
    Veggie Bowls with Coconut Lime Parsley Sauce, 202
Socca Flatbread, 151
sole fillets: Crispy Brown Butter Sole with Herby Green Rice, 187
soup
    Chilled Cucumber Gazpacho, 163
    Cozy Roasted Parsnip Soup, 129
    Cozy Sausage and Lentil Stew, 169
    Healthy Veggie Noodle Pho, 132
    The Italian Situation, 199
    Poblano Chicken Tortilla Soup, 205
    Roasted Kabocha Squash Soup, 135
    Sweet Potato Turkey Chili, 200
    3-Ingredient Tomato Soup, 131
Special Burger Sauce, 189
The Spicy Cabo, 248
Spicy Chicken Burgers or Meatballs, 188
Spicy Cilantro Mule, 248
Spicy Tomato Shakshuka, 76
spinach
    Butternut Squash and Sage Risotto, 193
    Chocolate Green Smoothies, 49
    The Morning Warming Smoothie, 53
spirulina powder
    Spirulina Energy Balls, 138
    Superfood Butter and Banana Bites, 143
squash
    The Anytime Breakfast Bowl, 61
    Butternut Squash and Cardamom Pancakes, 84
    Butternut Squash and Sage Risotto, 193
    Kale and Quinoa Salad with Squash, Apricots, and Bacon, 127
    Roasted Kabocha Squash Soup, 135
    Summer Picnic Poblano Salad, 105
    Supereasy Energy Balls, 138
    Superfood Butter and Banana Bites, 143
sweet potatoes
    The Fall Salad You Won't Be Able to Quit, 124
    The Morning Warming Smoothie, 53

Sweet Potato Morning Muffins, 70
Sweet Potato Turkey Chili, 200
Sweet Potato Waffles with Fried Eggs, 80
See also yams
Swiss chard leaves: Broccoli, Basil, and Goat Cheese Pizzas, 184

T
tahini
    The Cutie Pink Hummus, 155
    Roasted Cauliflower, Carrot, and Tahini Salad, 120
tamari: Carrot Noodle Pad Thai, 173
Thai Crab Cucumber Salad, 128
3-Ingredient Tomato Soup, 131
tomatoes
    The Cobb Job Salad, 110
    Green Bean, Cantaloupe, and Basil Salad, 214
    The Italian Situation, 199
    Pesto, Quinoa, and Tomato Salad, 106
    Poblano Chicken Tortilla Soup, 205
    The Real Greek Salad, 100
    Salmon Niçoise Salad with Sarah's Daily Basil Dressing, 102
    Seared Ahi and Crab Ceviche, 119
    The Sister A.G.T.O. Salad, 123
    Spicy Tomato Shakshuka, 76
    Sweet Potato Turkey Chili, 200
    Thai Crab Cucumber Salad, 128
    3-Ingredient Tomato Soup, 131
    Tomato Salad with Feta and Pistachios, 218
tomato paste: Bloody Mary Shrimp Cocktail, 160
tomato sauce
    Crustless Chicken Sausage and Veggie Pizza, 167
    Gigante Bean and Tomato Bake, 194
tortillas: Huevos Rancheros Bake, 90
tuna. See ahi tuna
turkey bacon
    The Cobb Job Salad, 110
    Kale and Quinoa Salad with Squash, Apricots, and Bacon, 127
turkey sausage
    Cozy Sausage and Lentil Stew, 169
    Turkey Sausage and Veggie Polenta Bowls, 190

V
vanilla bean: Vanilla Cold Brew, 32
vanilla extract
    Apple Pie Bars, 83
    Blackberry Scones, 86
    Cinnamon Chocolate Energy Balls, 142
    Chocolate Chip Olive Oil Cookies, 235
    Coconut and Cocoa Nib Balls, 141
    Cranberry Walnut Grain-Free Granola, 65
    Date Hot Chocolate, 36

Flourless Brownies, 231
Flourless Chocolate Crinkle Cookies, 236
Flourless Everything Cookies, 224
Healthy Crispy Rice Bars, 232
Healthy Pumpkin Spice Latte, 35
Homemade Nut Milk, 42
Honey Butter and Oatmeal Breakfast Cookies, 59
Life-Changing Gluten-Free Waffles, 89
Maca Hot Chocolate, 36
Matcha Vanilla Energy Balls, 138
Mini Pumpkin Spice Doughnuts (or Muffins), 75
Seasonal Jam Dots, 62
Snickerdoodle Energy Balls, 138
Spirulina Energy Balls, 138
Sweet Potato Morning Muffins, 70
Vanilla Apricot Granola Bars, 144
Veggie Bowls with Coconut Lime Parsley Sauce, 202

W
walnuts
    Cranberry Walnut Grain-Free Granola, 65
    The Everyday Chicken Salad, 109
    Kale Feta Bread, 94
    Vanilla Apricot Granola Bars, 144
The Warm Shaved Brussels Sprout Caesar, 171
Whipped Feta Dip, 152
Winter Greens Gratin, 196

Y
yams
    The Fall Salad You Won't Be Able to Quit, 124
    Sweet Potato Morning Muffins, 70
    Sweet Potato Turkey Chili, 200
    See also sweet potatoes
yogurt
    Baja Chopped Caesar Salad, 116
    Kale Feta Bread, 94
    1-Minute Miracle Sauce, 189
    Savory Yogurt Bowls, 66
    Whipped Feta Dip, 152

Z
zucchini
    Crustless Chicken Sausage and Veggie Pizza, 167
    Healthy Veggie Noodle Pho, 132
    Mint Chocolate Green Smoothie, 49
    The Morning Warming Smoothie, 53
    Spicy Chicken Burgers or Meatballs, 188
    Turkey Sausage and Veggie Polenta Bowls, 190
    Veggie Bowls with Coconut Lime Parsley Sauce, 202
    Zucchini Bread, 87

SARAH ADLER is a nutrition coach, healthy lifestyle expert, food blogger, real food lover, and owner of the lifestyle company, Simply Real Health. The author of *The Simply Real Health Cookbook*, her recipes have been featured by *Huffington Post*, *Well + Good*, *Cooking Light*, *Buzzfeed*, and *Woman's Day*. She lives in Seattle, Washington, with her husband and son.